Publicity, Newsletters, and Press Releases

Alison Baverstock is a well-known marketer who throughout her career has combined teaching with a successful marketing practice. As well as having wide experience as a trainer (including 12 years at The Publishing Training Centre at Book House), she has written two distance learning courses on promotional copy-writing and marketing, has experience as a distance learning tutor on the PTC copy-writing course, and has her own clients, ranging from many publishers, to a ski company, to charities. She is the author of *Marketing Your Book: an author's guide* (A & C Black, 2001), *How to Market Books* (Kogan Page, 1999), *Commonsense Marketing for Non-Marketers* (Piatkus, 1995), and *Are Books Different?* (Kogan Page, 1993).

One Step Ahead ...

The *One Step Ahead* series is for all those who want and need to communicate more effectively in a range of real-life situations. Each title provides up-to-date practical guidance, tips, and the language tools to enhance your writing and speaking.

Series Editor: John Seely

Acknowledgements

I would like to thank the following for their help:
Sarah Barrett, Derek Birdsall, Helen Cox, John Diamond, Cathy Douglas, Elizabeth Haddow, Peter Hobday, Jennifer and Helmut Gorlich, Paula Johnson, Nick Martin, Gill Morgan, Alysoun Owen, Cate Pedder, David Seabourne, Gerald Scott, Toby Scott, and John Seely.

Publicity, Newsletters, and Press Releases

Alison Baverstock

Cartoons by Beatrice Baumgartner-Cohen

OXFORD UNIVERSITY PRESS

Great Clarendon Street, Oxford OX2 6DP

Oxford University Press is a department of the University of Oxford.
It furthers the University's objective of excellence in research, scholarship,
and education by publishing worldwide in
Oxford New York
Auckland Bangkok Buenos Aires Cape Town Chennai
Dar es Salaam Delhi Hong Kong Istanbul Karachi Kolkata
Kuala Lumpur Madrid Melbourne Mexico City Mumbai Nairobi
São Paulo Shanghai Singapore Taipei Tokyo Toronto
with an associated company in Berlin

Oxford is a registered trade mark of Oxford University Press
in the UK and in certain other countries

Published in the United States
by Oxford University Press Inc., New York

British Library Cataloguing in Publication Data
Data available

Library of Congress Cataloging in Publication Data
Data available

ISBN 0-19-860384-3

10 9 8 7 6 5 4 3 2 1

Design and typesetting by David Seabourne
Printed in Spain by Bookprint S.L., Barcelona

Contents

1 | Introduction

Welcome. This book is one of a series of titles that looks at communication and how to get a message across effectively.

My particular concern in this title is how to generate publicity and promote public relations through the effective use of words. The book is aimed at anyone who needs to publicize an organization or cause, whether multinational business or church fete. Whether you have to produce the words yourself, or make decisions on those written by other people, I hope you will find it useful.

What is the best way of communicating with your customers?

Almost every organization, whether public or private, depends on customers or supporters, and needs to communicate with them on a regular basis. But deciding how best to get a message across can be problematic.

Let's begin by thinking about the options that exist for getting a message across. The most obvious examples to spring to mind are those in which **you pay for inclusion**.

An option considered early by most organizations is **space advertising**, or paying for an advertisement in the medium of your choice, perhaps a newspaper or magazine.

'The medium is the message.'
Marshall McLuhan

But space advertising is expensive, and given the current fragmentation of the media (there are lots of new formats being launched all the time, each one offering slightly different market segmentation and penetration), it can be difficult to decide how best to reach the market.

Advertisements can be enjoyable to the reader, and bring a product to their notice very effectively in this way. But you should also bear in mind that the very fact that a message is communicated through space advertising means that its content may be downgraded by the reader, because it will be assumed to be partisan—no organization will use the space in its advertisements to tell you objectively what it is *really* like.

Another option growing in popularity is **direct marketing**, or the sending of a sales message directly to the customer, whether through the post, via a telephone call, or by a house-to-house visit. Direct marketing has grown hugely in recently years and is now challenging the amount of money spent on space advertising. Many organizations like using direct marketing because it offers greater measurability than space advertising. As the marketing communication asks the customer to respond directly (perhaps through a reply-paid order form or telephone line), the effectiveness of each campaign can be analysed and lessons learnt in the process fed into the next communication.

Other marketing solutions include arranging **promotions** (linking products in a joint promotion such as collecting crisp packet tokens towards new books for a school library) and **competitions** (a children's colouring competition to choose the design for the mayor's next Christmas card).

Many organizations rely on personal contact with the market, sending out **representatives** to demonstrate the products or take orders.

It is important to note that none of the above forms of marketing communication are mutually exclusive: lots of organizations use a variety, or all of them, in various combinations. So a direct mailshot to a market may be followed up by representatives telephoning those who received it, or copies of planned space advertising will be sent to reps for them to point out to customers they are visiting during the same period.

Controlling the message

The advantage that all these methods of communication offer is that you mostly have control of what is said about you. To take the example of a sales brochure or space advertisement, the commissioner writes the copy—or gets it written—and pays for design, print, postage, and circulation costs.

'Unless one is a genius, it is best to aim at being intelligible.'

Anthony Hope

In return, you are guaranteed to reach a certain number of people; advertising managers can quote circulation and readership figures; companies which provide mailing lists can give you a total of the named individuals reached.

The difference between circulation figures and being read

What suppliers cannot guarantee, however, is how many of those you target with your information *will actually read it*. And there can be a huge difference between those who have access to, or personally receive, your information and those who absorb your message.

An advertisement in a magazine or newspaper may be flicked past; a mailshot may be binned on receipt. An organization may make a corporate decision not to see sales representatives any more, or decide that promotions waste their customers' time and run them no more.

There can be a huge difference between those who have access to your information and those who read your message.

Free publicity: how to be part of the medium you choose

One subject of this book is how to communicate with those who have media space at their disposal, and can offer your organisation coverage without a resulting invoice—what is commonly known as **free publicity**.

This is really a strange term, for whilst your effort may result in no invoice, free publicity takes an enormous amount of time to organize effectively. You must send the information you would like to see included to those who have space/air time at their disposal. It's a good idea to present the information in a way likely to appeal to their interests, and as a result you can hope that positive coverage will result. But never forget that, in the process, you give up control of what is said about you.

Free publicity

Although you don't pay for it, free publicity takes an enormous amount of time to organize effectively.

Overcoming a fear of getting involved in publicity and public relations

Involvement in publicity and PR can be offputting to many. If you are occupied running a business, you may have little extra time to put into handling good relations with journalists, and be very fearful of what they might write about you. News journalists have a terrible reputation:

> They are, it is alleged, an egocentric, single-minded, cynical, unforgiving bunch who have only one wish in life and that is to dig the dirt and ruin your reputation, regardless of the facts
>
> Peter Hobday, broadcaster and former presenter of the Today Programme

Involvement in publicity and PR can be off-putting to many. News journalists have a terrible reputation.

These fears are very common. You probably worry about:

■ Unscrupulous journalists who will distort your message.

■ Being misunderstood.

■ Instructing professionals, because it will cost a fortune. Added to this may be uncertainty about how to judge whether what external suppliers produce is effective or not.

■ A lack of understanding about how journalists work and what kind of stories they need.

At the same time, most organizations have a desire to make the most of the opportunities for free publicity that do occur. Some organizations seem to get coverage all the time (Richard Branson's Virgin, Anita Roddick's Body Shop) and it's natural to want to save money spent on advertizing and see similar benefits for your own organization.

Help is at hand

Take heart. This book will help you. Here you will find very simple techniques that you can learn in order to maximize your chances of positive coverage. I will show you how to present ideas so that they have the strongest chance of being picked up and used by journalists.

The approach will be systematic. You will be encouraged to think about what journalists need to know and what kind of media to approach, and how best to present your information, in both style and format.

'The object of oratory is not truth but persuasion.'

Thomas Babington Macaulay

I will describe the working situation of journalists so that you know when to approach them and what kind of information you should provide about yourself and your organization. If you understand the motivation and goals of those you are working with, you are more likely to be able to harness them to your own best interests.

There will be many examples, from a variety of different sources, so that you can see how the suggestions work in practice.

Above all, a precise and targeted approach will be advocated. Despite all indications to the contrary, planning for publicity and press coverage is a precise activity, not a random one. My aim is to produce a more confident writer, better able to judge what the impact of their words will be, and hence to shape the desired outcome.

2

Why using the right language is so important

This book deals with producing printed communications, from newsletters and press releases to a variety of different kinds of publicity material. You will learn about what each format usually consists of, when it should most logically be used, and how to make what you say really effective.

In this chapter I want to make two simple but important points, both of which I will illustrate with lots of examples. I then want to talk about how to prepare yourself to write effectively.

Printed communications have authority

Printed communications are a formal expression of an organization: what it is like and what it wants or tries to do. Never forget this.

Remember:
Leaflets and press releases represent your organization, and can enhance or damage a company's reputation.

It's tempting to think of your printed communications in much more straightforward terms. For example, a leaflet is there to explain what you do, a press release to tell the media what you have planned. But in reality, these pieces of paper represent your organization to the outside world in a very formal way, and they will carry on doing so until those who take an interest in you decide otherwise.

So who does take an interest in you? Depending on what kind of organization you are involved with, you will most likely have a band of customers/existing clients and/or supporters who will be pleased to hear from you. But there is a much wider range of people you may reach, some of whom you may prefer *not* to read your information at all. For example, what you send out may be read by:

There is a much wider range of people you may reach, whose motivation is less easy to predict and provide for, and some of whom you may prefer not to read your information at all

- Your shareholders (who may be making a connection between the amount spent on communicating with them and the financial dividend they eventually receive). The governors, directors, and trustees of non-profit-making organizations may respond in this way too.

- Your existing customers and supporters. Remember this group will almost certainly include a number who have 'itchy feet' and are considering a change. This is even more likely if they are new to their job and want to be seen as a 'new broom'. You need to be careful to avoid providing them with the justification for change.

- Those who might like to work or get involved with you in the future, and who are keeping an eye on you until they see the right job or project advertised.

- Your existing employees/volunteers (who will be particularly quick to spot if there is a gap between what you claim to offer and what you actually deliver).

- Your local community.

- Your competitors.

- Your enemies (in these days of the 'leak' for monetary or political advantage, you should never have an argument in print unless you are happy to be quoted).

✗ Don't!

have an argument in print unless you are happy to be quoted.

- The press (who may sniff out the story you *don't* want explored from the information you *do* put out).

This may sound intimidating, and is not designed to make you do nothing at all. Rather, I just want to warn you to be careful of the impression you create in print.

The more formal the communication vehicle you choose, the greater will be the standard of presentation expected

The standard of presentation expected by your market will vary according to the communication medium you choose to get your message across. The more formal the vehicle you choose, the higher will be their expectations. Here are some examples to prove this point.

" Ye Poore Scholar "

Starter's:
Pumkin Soap
Tomatoe Salad
Main Corse's:
Beefstake w. Roast Potatos
Dover Soul w. Beens
Desert
Chokolate Moose

Blackboards and printed menus in restaurants

Many restaurants offer a blackboard on which staff chalk up 'dishes of the day'. Spelling mistakes and words missed out will probably occur in the process, because it's very difficult to write on a surface that is vertical rather than the more usual horizontal, and using a much larger size of lettering may lead to errors. The market will, however, probably be tolerant.

But when it comes to the printed menu that gets handed out by the waiting staff, very different standards will be expected. This is not the place to advertise that you can't spell the dishes that you promise to be able to make, or to use casual grammar.

Emails and text for publication

Email provides a very fast and flexible method of communication; ideas can be dispatched quickly and there is usually more emphasis on the idea and the person to whom it is being speedily despatched than on the standard of language it contains. When it comes to text for website or printed publication, however, the email user must raise their standards from casual to very precise.

The following extract, which confirms my point, is from a tribute by the editor of the *Times Magazine*, Gill Morgan, to her former columnist John Diamond, who had just died of throat

Emails

With an email there is usually more emphasis on the idea and the person to whom it is being sent than on the standard of language it contains. This is never true of text to be printed.

cancer. He wrote a regular column for the magazine in which he charted the progress of his disease, which eventually robbed him of his voice. She is talking here of the contrast between the notes he sent her by email and the copy for the columns which they would accompany.

> Email meant he could retain his eloquence and quick wit and voice, and it enabled us both—in the way that email is peculiarly well-equipped to do—to roam between the most serious of conversations and the most flippant. He would occasionally tag on the odd message at the top of his column. Some of it is the dull, dull talk of deadlines; some of it urgent requests for gossip (normally after a stint in hospital—'Gossip me up' he'd tap); some of it slurred and misspelt (but he never, ever misspelt anything in his copy) as he struggled through morphine or sometimes the aftermath of a raucous night out.

Thus email is the medium of informal communication in which errors are acceptable according to how well you know the recipient, but formal articles for publication demand much more exacting standards.

Handwritten and typed letters

A handwritten letter is the most personal form of written communication. The recipient may tolerate misspellings or words missed out as they are swept along in an understanding of *what the sender meant to say*.

But if you imagine the same letter typed, then errors will leap out at the reader, and no latitude will be given. Misspellings may not be clear when handwritten, but will be very obvious when the same words are typed, because there is then no mistaking the individual letters.

What is more, the spacing of the words, the length of the paragraphs, and the type of paper used become part of the message. Whether or not the recipient realizes it, they will be making subconscious judgements about the sender based on the standards of presentation.

Presentation and communication

Most formal
↓
Handwritten letter
↓
Email
↓
Least formal

Preparing yourself to write well

The difference between producing copy and writing

'Copy' is words that are used to get a message across.

All the above examples require the effective use of words, but when used in the context described, we are talking about producing 'copy' rather than 'writing'. 'Copy' is words that are used to get a message across.

An essay produced for teachers at school or college differs from the kind of promotional writing we are now talking about, for one fundamental reason: the recipient has to read it in order to mark it.

The recipient of copy has every choice: they may decide to read what you send, but equally they may decide to bin it, use it as scrap paper, or put it under a cup of coffee.

Promotional writing is difficult

Writing is often seen as easy; it's a basic skill learnt at school which everyone must master. But producing effective copy is immensely difficult. Here are a few reasons why:

- Whilst everyone can write, not everyone can get a message —or the right message—across.

It's a travesty your majesty

The Sun, 21 December 2001

- It is far more difficult to draft an effective short sentence than a long one. Ironically, it will often be assumed that the opposite is the case. The shorter the final copy, the harder it will be to produce it. That's why the best-paid headline writers in newspapers work on *The Sun* and *The Mirror* rather than *The Times* and *The Guardian*.

Unflinching, unsmiling, the Queen surrenders to the bleak gaze of a painter unschooled in the flatterer's art

The Times, 21 December 2001

- Even if you can produce words quickly, it is vital that copy is both error-free and unambiguous. Thus copy should always be checked and rechecked to ensure it is correct.

Allow enough time to do the job properly

The correct drafting of text takes time. Remember that the copy drafted will be reviewed and interpreted over a much longer period, so it's important to allow enough time for its creation. Poorly drafted or ambiguous printed information about your organization can come back to haunt you. To paraphrase the proverb, 'Act in haste, repent at leisure.'

Don't expect to be able to produce copy all day long.

Don't expect to be able to produce copy all day long. Effective copywriting takes great creativity, and no one can be creative all the time. It's vital to take regular breaks from writing, to allow thinking space to review and revise.

I find I get some of my best ideas when I am not at my desk. Having done all the background reading for the subject you are to write about, let it sit in your brain and allow the important message to come forth. I find I have some good ideas when I am in surroundings that are nothing to do with work: on trains or in the bath! Keep a cassette recorder or pad and pencil handy.

You should avoid having to finalize words on the same day you draft them. Always try to leave what you have written for a few days (overnight is better than nothing) before sending off/passing onto those who will organize production. Ideas or phrases

Stages in producing copy

Background reading

Thinking time

Draft text

Thinking again

Review

Rewrite and finalize

that seem funny at the end of one afternoon may be completely lost in the cold light of the next morning. Awkward sentence construction or words that are overused often don't show up when you are writing, but will leap out at you if you come back to them after a few days. Keep a running file of everything you have ever written, and you will find that work from a few years ago seems to belong to someone else.

And once you have finished ...

Being objective about copy you have worked on very closely on is difficult. So once you have finished:

- Read it aloud. Copy that is difficult to read aloud will be even more difficult to read in the head. Look out in particular for sentences that are too long, or need punctuation, and the overuse of adjectives (are they too predictable, too difficult, or simply too many?).

- Get someone who knows nothing about the project to read it through. Do they understand? In the world of newspapers, the sub-editor has a very important place. It is they who check the copy provided by journalists and feature writers to ensure that it is easy to read. It is significant that very few journalists are allowed to write and then sub-edit their own material.

- Ask *someone else* to read it aloud. Remember your reader will be coming to it fresh and will not have the opportunity of a 'warm-up'. This is not for the faint-hearted, but can be a wonderful way of finding out whether or not your copy is easy to read.

- If you are checking the copy of a subordinate, try to be really sure that the changes you make are there because they really need making, rather than proof of your own need to demonstrate that *you* are the manager.

Stages in checking copy

Read text aloud.

Get feedback from an outside source.

Ask someone else to read it aloud.

One final point

Think clearly about *who* should write copy, as and when it
is needed.

It's a good idea to accept the principle that writing is a gift, and
to get the person within your organization with the largest
quota of that gift to do the writing. This can be difficult if you
are the manager, and you are forced in the process to recognize
that one of your subordinates is better at it than you are, but
your organization will be the long-term beneficiary. Delegation
is a very important part of management, and in the process you
will be raising the profile of public information and insisting
that everyone takes it seriously.

3

Getting it right: a short guide to promotional writing

'*Syllables govern the world.*'

John Selden

'*Only connect!*'

E. M. Forster

Introduction

Having established the importance of promotional writing, this chapter will look at the mechanics of putting your text together: from individual words to how to make a sentence really effective. In subsequent chapters we will then look at how to construct the promotional materials that are the subject of this book.

Words: the basic building blocks

The words you use play a huge part in the audience's readiness to read and absorb your message.

Talk about 'you' rather than 'me'

I remember my English teacher at school explaining that the secret of writing a good letter is to talk about the person you are writing to rather than yourself. Since then I have decided that this is a principle that holds good whatever you are writing: effective writing starts with thinking about who will be reading what you say. Customers are far more interested in their own needs and problems than your organization's achievements, so news about the latter always needs to be presented from the recipient's point of view.

One easy, if rather crude, way of measuring how focused your copy is on the market is to count the number of first- and second-person pronouns in the piece (i.e. the number of *I/we* to the number of *you*). There should be far more of the latter than the former. Alternatively, as someone pithily put it:

> You have two ears and one mouth. They should be used in the same proportion.

Pay attention to the sensitivities (or 'isms') of your market

Everyone has sensitive issues to which they are particularly attuned: sexism, racism, ageism, and so on. These will change as your life circumstances change.

For example, new parents pushing prams suddenly notice how pavements become difficult to walk along when cars park on them; when their child starts to walk they often become very anti-dog fouling and pro-play spaces; later, issues of education and access concern them. Similarly, in the world of work, current sensitivities will range from the professional (salaries, safety, employment trends) to those based on intrigue and gossip (who has been sacked and from what, who has been headhunted, and who is having an affair with whom).

As a writer who is seeking to get a message across to a target group, it is essential to understand the '-isms' that affect all those you are writing to, and to reflect these in the vocabulary you use. If you are using illustrations, you need to ensure that the pictures chosen reinforce your words.

For example, one of the most burning issues in schools today is equality of opportunity. Schools are required to have a written policy on how to implement it and are thus acutely conscious of bias. If you send information to schools on a new range of sports resources and refer to or show them only being used by boys, your message will not be as well received as possible. Along the same lines, never assume that all nurses are female, or business people male. You will alienate your readers if you fail to think about their sensitivities.

'Words are, of course, the most powerful drug used by mankind.'
Rudyard Kipling

Watch out!
not to offend:

different races or nationalities

different sexes

different sexual orientations

3 Getting it right:
a short guide to
promotional writing

How can you find out about the sensitivities of a market?

Read the 'trade press'—the name commonly given to the professional publications in a particular field. For example, nurses have *Nursing Times* and in the book trade, *The Bookseller* and *Publishing News* are widely read. If you don't understand the articles, read the letters pages and the job advertisements.

Try to talk to members of your target market, starting with any that you know personally. Ask what information they get sent, and which items they respond well to. It can be particularly instructive to hear about promotional approaches that annoy them, and to ask the reasons why. Find out about exhibitions and conferences that are being organized in your field and try to attend. Once there, listen to as many conversations as possible and pick up other organizations' promotional brochures.

Use words that are easy to understand

Most people read promotional copy quickly, so the shorter the words, the clearer the message. The same is true for your sentence structure. Start with a short sentence; thereafter vary your sentence length to avoid monotony. Don't use long phrases where single words will do. For example:

Use	Instead of
Most	A great deal
Key	Widely acclaimed
Now	At the current moment in time

'The most valuable of our talents is that of never using two words where one will do.'

Thomas Jefferson

Try to use short words rather than long ones. As Mark Twain wrote:

I never write metropolis for seven cents because I can get the same price for city. I never write policeman because I can get the same money for cop.

Following his example:

Use	Instead of
Find	Discover
News, facts	Information
Now	Immediately
Show	Demonstrate

On the other hand the occasional long word can be very effective, particularly if it is surrounded by shorter words which throw it into greater prominence:

a monstrous carbuncle on the face of a much loved friend

Use words that are interesting

Do not write exactly what your market expects. If a reader can guess the content they may not bother to read what you send. Good copy conveys a slightly unexpected message. Try to use words that are vivid and interesting, rather than predictable.

Try	Rather than
Huge	Major
Nailbiting	Exciting
Tragic	Sad
Rush	Despatch
Tough	Difficult

'The chief virtue that language can have is clearness.'
Hippocrates

'An original writer is not one who imitates nobody, but one whom nobody can imitate.'
Vicomte de Chateaubriand

23

3 Getting it right:
a short guide to
promotional writing

Avoid hackneyed terms

Language is not static; words change their meaning all the time, both through overuse and new developments. In some sectors of society (such as adolescents) these changes may be extremely rapid, but in every group there will be words that get used too often and hence lose their impact.

Check the trade press for the area you are writing for, looking out for words and phrases that get used too often. Here are a few to watch out for and not use too often:

> Timely; useful; unique; invaluable; exciting; outstanding; accessible

'The purpose of newspeak is to make all other modes of thought impossible.'

George Orwell.

Check on the number of adjectives you use

At school we were encouraged to use adjectives to develop our writing, and this tradition has spilled over into promotional copy to the point where no noun is seen as complete unless it has two accompanying adjectives. For example:

> perfect and convenient location

> useful and timely book

✔ **Do!**

be original

be unpredictable

be flexible

Watch out!
For words you use too often yourself. I must confess to: *hugely, vital,* and *key.*

Your writing may have more impact if you miss out the adjectives all together, or have just one, or even three. Just ring the changes; if every noun has two, the prose is leaden.

Avoid jargon and slang

Jargon is best defined as in-house talk: terms that mean something to those involved in an area, but nothing to those outside it. Whilst it is tempting to use it, to show you understand the market you are writing for, resist the temptation, because:

'Slang is a language that rolls up its sleeves, spits on its hands, and goes to work.'

Carl Sandburg

■ it changes all the time, so you cannot be sure of being current;

■ your text will not be understood by those new to the profession, and you will alienate them.

The same goes for slang, which can date very quickly.

Common misspellings and misinterpretations

**3 Getting it right:
a short guide to
promotional writing**

There are words that sound alike or are similar, and are commonly confused (for example *affect/effect*; *principal/principle*). Use a dictionary if you are not sure how a particular word should be spelt. Be aware that, even if you are using a word processor with a spell-checking facility, it may not be picking up words that are real ones, but in the wrong place:

*Beware spell-
checker!*

> My computer has a spell cheque. It lives on my pea sea.

Ensure your spell-check does not change words that do not need changing. This often happens with names.

Check up on your grammar

The teaching of grammar has gone in and out of fashion in recent years. At times rigorous attention to sentence construction has been seen as a barrier to creativity, at other times as essential to any form of communication. Depending on when you left school, and what kind of school you went to, you may be more or less comfortable with the basics of grammar.

For basic guidance on the parts of speech, there is another title in this series which you should consult (*One Step Ahead: Words*). The following is a list of pitfalls which are particularly annoying to readers.

■ Ensure your **tenses** are consistent

Don't switch from one to the other, as in the following example of colloquial speech:

> The man rushed past and I say to my neighbour ...

should read:

> The man rushed past and I said to my neighbour ...

As a general rule, I try to write promotional text in the present tense:

> I am writing to you now to tell you about ...

rather than

> I wanted to write to you to tell you about ...

**3 Getting it right:
a short guide to
promotional writing**

■ Don't mix up plurals and singulars

If you are using a plural noun, then the verb should match it; don't switch from one to the other as in the following example:

We was very pleased to be invited.

Should read:

We were very pleased to be invited.

There is one exception to this rule, which is that it is increasingly acceptable to use a plural verb with a single noun if in the process you are able to include both genders.

The average eight-year-old will love this book; they will really appreciate the action packed story.

The supermarket customer needs to think very carefully before parking their car in a disabled parking spot.

■ Get the **apostrophe** right

The apostrophe is there to show either possession or that one or more letters have been missed out, for example:

The boy's pen. (possession)

Don't even think about it. (the 'o' has been missed out)

But you don't need an apostrophe in plural words such as *tomatoes* or *1990s*. The misuse of the apostrophe enrages many people, and may cause them to stop reading what is otherwise perfect wording.

■ Get **less** and **fewer** the right way round

You should use 'fewer' if you can count it, 'less' if you can't:

Fewer games of football took place last Saturday due to rain.

There was much less football played last season due to rain.

■ Avoid using the **split infinitive**

This is not because it is wrong, but because most people assume it to be so.

**3 Getting it right:
a short guide to
promotional writing**

In English the infinitive is always two words (e.g. *to love*) and many people believe that these two words should never be separated. The most famous example of a split infinitive is in the opening of *Star Trek*, when the Star Ship Enterprise's five-year mission is described:

To boldly go where no man has gone before.

Although there is nothing technically wrong with the split infinitive, because it is so easy to spot, and so widely held to be wrong, it is best to avoid it.

In all European languages apart from English, the infinitive is a single word.

Infinitive	Translation
aimer	Is the French for 'to love'
lieben	Is the German for 'to love'
amare	Is the Italian for 'to love'

Promotional writers have more fun!

'When I use a word, it means just what I choose it to mean—neither more nor less.'

Lewis Carroll

Writing to get a message across gives you a certain amount of freedom in your use of language; techniques which would have drawn adverse comment at school become acceptable in the wider aim of getting your copy noticed. For example, in promotional writing it is possible to:

 Do!

feel free to break some of the long-held 'rules' of grammar.

■ start a sentence with '**and**' or '**but**'. An arresting start can make a huge difference to whether or not your text gets read. If you are questioned about this, quote the Bible: 'And on the seventh day God rested.'

Don't!

break 'rules' because you don't know the correct usage.

3 **Getting it right:**
a short guide to
promotional writing

miss out key parts of the sentence if the construction makes sense without it. Single word sentences and imperatives can be particularly effective for headings and subheadings, for example:

Get going now!

Why?

use an exclamation mark and question mark at the same time:

Watch out?!

use colloquial (spoken) English:

Keep your shirt on!

Don't panic!

The unforgivable sin in promotional writing is to break grammatical rules without realizing it. Casual use of English grammar can alienate those who might otherwise be interested in your message.

Putting words together to build up your text

Effective copy should flow: smoothly leading the reader through your arguments and so to your desired outcome, whether that is the purchase of something you are selling or conversion to your point of view.

What you say should be as clear as possible. The best way of achieving this is to think *before* you write rather than as you write.

Think about the format you will choose. How will those you address find it easiest to absorb your message; press release, or telephone call?

Consider the appropriate tone. What is the best way of talking to your market?

Prepare a plan for what you will say in each paragraph, one theme per paragraph and one idea per sentence.

'The best argument is that which seems merely an explanation.'

Dale Carnegie

3 **Getting it right:
a short guide to
promotional writing**

■ You don't need to use every argument you have thought of in what you present; a couple of really strong points may be more effective than half a dozen.

■ Try to adopt a tone of sweet reason; a line of argument that progresses logically. It's difficult to resist.

Linking phrases are very useful in making the copy run smoothly, and hence carrying your reader with you.
For example:

After all ...	Did you realize ...	What's more ...
And of course ...	Just as important ...	Finally, I must just mention ...
At the same time ...	On the other hand ...	

How much should I write?

If you are asked to prepare copy, then 'how much copy?' is an obvious early question. Professional writers and journalists get used to being asked for round numbers. For example, a standard feature article in a quality paper is around 2,500 words. This book is about 20,000 words and a popular novel may be around 60,000.

For a new writer, rather than starting by thinking about how many words are needed, it is more helpful to think about what the words are required to do: in what context they will appear, who will be reading them, and how much time/inclination to read they have at their disposal. Look at how others have used the same amount of space, count the number of words used both in the headline (large type at the top) and the 'body copy' (text underneath). Work out the average number of words in the space and then think about whether more impact could have been created if:

Calculate ...

average words per
line x lines per page.

■ fewer words had been used, perhaps making them much larger and easier to read;

**3 Getting it right:
a short guide to
promotional writing**

*'Don't talk unless
you can improve
the silence.'*

Vermont proverb

see Part B for
advice on how to
divide up text

■ fewer ideas had been used, perhaps using the space instead to repeat (in different words) and hence reinforce a key message;

■ the words had been laid out in a more eye-catching design, with subheadings and space to 'signpost' the text and draw attention to key parts of the message;

■ the words had been presented as 'advertorial', i.e. mimicking the style and presentation of a familiar publication or the one in which they are to appear rather than looking like an advertisement. Your writing style will have to match the relevant image, but more readers may result.

Not including every idea you think of

You don't need to use every sales benefit you have thought of. If you include too much information, you may end up confusing your potential customers.

For example, representatives of window replacement services regularly knock on our front door. Leaflets spelling out the benefits of what they offer usually mention the following:

■ a warmer house as double glazing cuts down draughts and heat loss;

■ improved security as burglars will find it harder to break in;

■ improving the appearance of the property;

■ investing in our property, so it is worth more should we decide to sell it;

■ a special offer to encourage us to talk right now (a free survey on existing windows or money off/added value).

But were the representative to offer all these at the beginning of a conversation, you would quickly grow bored. Most choose one of the above as a 'tempter'.

The buying reasons of your customers may be different from your own

Remember that your own reasons for doing what you do may not be same as those of your market. For example, a friend of mine was involved recently with a local theatre which was trying to boost support in the immediate area. Productions are of an extremely high standard, and this is what motivates the director and actors. But when it comes to the audience, whilst this is important, there are other reasons they enjoy attending. In particular, they liked:

■ Supporting a local venture.
 Locals enjoyed patronizing a local enterprise; being part of a theatre-going community which both enhanced the area they lived in and got them to meet like-minded people.

■ Ease of access.
 For local people the theatre is easy to drive and walk to. What is more, the short distance home afterwards means you can enjoy an evening out midweek without feeling exhausted the next day.

4 | Publicity

What is publicity?

The most obvious definition of publicity is that of 'making public': keeping the name of the product/service/person, or whatever is being promoted, in the public mind. The aim of publicity is to usually to achieve sales or boost recognition *at a specific time*; there is little point in achieving publicity before the product in question is available for purchase in the shops, or before the person you are publicizing is available for interview in this country.

Is there any such thing as bad publicity?

The popular view that there is no such thing as bad publicity rather depends on the industry you are talking about, and where the publicity takes place. The US reaction to Hugh Grant's arrest in Hollywood for employing the services of a prostitute was that it was a publicity stunt: stars would rather be talked about than not talked about.

Honey, there's no such thing as bad publicity

In other areas of activity this may be less true; journalists like a story that will run and run (one 'with legs', as they term it), and a negative story can be picked up and developed just as enthusiastically as a positive one. For example, the problems of

British Gas in the 1990s, the Dome in the year 2000, or the declining fortunes of Marks and Spencer were examples of long-running negative stories, where one bad story led to the next: the public appetite was ever-ready for the next tale of disaster.

Why bother trying to achieve publicity?

There are several main reasons.

■ It is free.

Publicity coverage in the media, whether broadcast or printed, does not result in an invoice for the space/time taken. With advertising rates in the media rising, and the number of different outlets available sectioning the market (and hence making it very difficult to identify media that get to a broad range of the public), this is very useful.

■ It becomes part of the publication.

If a journalist covers your story, then information will appear as part of the publication rather than part of the advertising.

There is a clear subliminal message here. Information that is in advertising format will be assumed to be partisan, whereas if the story is part of the news or feature coverage, the reporting is much more likely to be accepted. In other words, free publicity gives you a much higher credibility with your audience than space you have paid for.

> Information that is in advertising format will be assumed to be partisan.

What is more, if your information is printed by a paper as editorial text, you can then quote what they print with *their* name at the bottom of it in your future marketing materials. An effective endorsement is a very powerful tool in marketing. Sending a well-crafted piece of information to a journalist, which they then endorse by using whole, effectively allows you to write your own reviews.

> This is the reason why some advertisers layout their advertising text as editorial; often referred to as an 'advertorial' or an 'advertising feature'. Text that looks like editorial is more likely to be believed.

■ Advantageous timing is possible.

Releasing a story to the press at the time that suits you best can yield coverage in a medium that might have required booking months ahead for paid coverage at the same time. Orchestrating publicity also allows you to respond very quickly to news events, so either put your own point of view or include your organization in a story that is already running.

■ It's a valuable way of varying the tone from more formal marketing communications.

Even best-selling products can become boring to the market. Political changes within an organization, such as a change of management or a prominent failure/success of another initiative, may lead to a desire for change. An obvious way of achieving variety quickly is to change your supplier(s). Interestingly, it is apparently common practice for smokers trying to give up tobacco to change the brand of cigarettes they use instead.

Publicity offers you a valuable way of changing the tone of your organization's communications. For example, most newspapers offer 'diary' columns which feature snippets of interesting information, often about the people *behind* news stories. Mentions of serious issues and products in diary columns are thus a very effective way of broadening coverage, and are at the same time motivating for all concerned.

Example

As an instance of this in practice, for several years I promoted a range of high-level science journals for medical researchers. Each month I would receive a list of forthcoming papers for the next issue. I have very little understanding of science, so if I saw a forthcoming paper whose title I could understand, and which I felt had a human interest angle, I would feed the information to 'medical briefings' or diary columns in the broadsheet papers. The results were very powerful—the editorial team were delighted to be cited in the national press and we were sure the increased profile of the journals played a part in prompting other people to publish their research through them. Subscription levels rose.

What you have to give in return

Of course these advantages lead to a range of considerations that perhaps compromise what you want to achieve.

In return for the oxygen of free publicity, the journalist will be looking for something back.

Unless they are very short of material, and your press release extremely interesting, they will probably not print just what you send them. You will consequently have to target the story you send, to tamper with it to make it match *their* needs.

How is it best to go about this? You need to remember that rather than putting forward the objective truth at all times, all media serve to reinforce the prejudices of their regulars; that is how they keep their readership loyal and their publications bought/programmes watched or listened to. Newspaper editors and programme makers have access to accurate market research indicating who the audience is and what kind of interest/political bias/intellectual capacity they have. They will

> All media serve to reinforce the prejudices of their regulars.

The 'angle' is the way in which a story is tailored to meet the perceived needs of the audience.

Example

try to find the kind of stories that appeal to this particular audience and it follows that if yours is sympathetically presented, it may get an airing. Here is an example of how different angles of the same story can be developed to interest the readers of various newspapers.

> **Madonna in the News**
> Let's imagine a story about the pop singer Madonna, and how she spends the millions of dollars she has earned. This could appeal to many papers. For the Sun, there would be a sexy picture of the singer, and fewer words, but her millions would fascinate its readers. There might or might not be a picture of Madonna in the FT, but readers would be interested in what she was doing with her money, especially if she was doing something that other investors could benefit from. The women's page in the Guardian might picture her as a strong feminist icon; the home pages might feature her domestic expenses; the fashion page might focus on how much she spends on clothes and who are her chosen designers. There would also, no doubt, be paragraphs galore in the gossip columns.

Other caveats to bear in mind

■ You won't get publicity in every vehicle you want.

■ And not necessarily when you want.

Seeking publicity does not give you the right to select the angle chosen.

■ Or even the story you want. Seeking publicity does not give you the right to select the angle chosen. We have already discussed that most publicity aims to make something public, but the dictionary definition also refers to the pursuit of notoriety, which is a much stronger word. Not all public scrutiny is welcome.

'Damned to everlasting fame'

Alexander Pope

■ Having prompted a relationship with the press, they may go on contacting you when you wish they would go away. Celebrity can have its disadvantages too—never again can someone who has been in the news lead a quiet life.

What you need to pursue publicity

- a media strategy;

- a message that you want to put over and that the media will be interested in;

- a list of places (magazines, radio shows, etc.) you would like to be seen and relevant contacts to try and achieve that;

- something to send;

- a strategy for following up and keeping the momentum going.

> **Practical help:**
> - The Internet
> - Periodical Directories
> - Keep an ongoing database

A media strategy

What are you trying to do? Launch an overnight sensation or drip-feed information that will gradually increase your profile over the next three years? Before getting involved with the media, you need to think about this.

A message that the media will be interested in

If you want publicity, you have to have some news to tell. This has to be succinct, memorable, and easy to pass on.

In this context, what is news? Something that has a story at the bottom of it, that is easy to remember, and that people *want* to pass on—to tell their friends in the local pub or their partner when they get home.

In some cases the story will be ready-made. If you are forming a single-issue pressure group, for a playground on a newly built housing estate, or for a zebra crossing on a dangerous road, then the issue is already in place. You should, however, bear in mind that:

- The media are more interested in the specific than the general.

There may have been lots of people injured but the story of just one may capture their attention. The hook to catch the journalist's attention is often an individual, and on the back of their story you can broaden out to an issue. Personal information will be needed to illustrate your point—photographs, anecdotes, and much more.

If you are trying to get publicity for an organization or individual, then you will have to think around the subject and be both resourceful and succinct. Ask yourself the following questions:

- What is interesting/newsworthy about the project?

- Who do they know, who are their friends, are there any people who could provide a useful quote or endorsement?

- Who are their enemies? Have any spoken out publicly?

- Where do they live?

- Does the project represent something that is significant in society/a growing trend?

Now, try to answer answer each of these questions briefly, and using a vocabulary that reflects your enthusiasm for the subject. For example, thinking of a local campaign for a zebra crossing, instead of:

Mary Smith has walked children to school for twenty years and seen many near-accidents on the way.

try:

You try

Mary Smith dreads walking children to school. Over the twenty years she has done so, she has seen countless near-accidents as drivers race along the Richmond Road.

The second example is much more emotive and consequently conveys a much stronger mental image. The specific detail quoted adds reality and would greatly appeal to a local paper.

Often the attention of the press will be attracted by details which the individual at the centre of a story takes for granted, but which, looked at in a more interesting way, or in comparison with the rest of the world, are fascinating. For example, a worker for a charity involved with the Third World told friends, in a very matter of fact way, that she had moved roughly once a year for the past twenty years. This did not strike her as unusual, but it sent shock waves through others listening.

Targeting media and contacts

Make a list of all the media where you would like to see your story appear. By all means start with those you know of yourself, but then try to think more widely. Who else might be interested? For inspiration, consult a press guide (you will find a variety of different ones in the reference section of your local library). Be sure to include the local media—television, radio, and press—rather than just concentrating on the nationals. Large-size papers such as *The Times* and *The Telegraph* are known generically as the 'broadsheets', or colloquially as the 'quality press'. The smaller, picture-based papers such as *The Mirror* and *The Sun* are referred to as the 'tabloids'.

See Part B, Checklist for writing a press release.

For each medium you wish to contact, get hold of a copy of the most recent issue/watch the programme and find out the name of the spot or feature you wish to be included in. Then ring up to find out the name of the relevant news/features editor. News editors deal with what is current, features editors look to create or commission more considered background pieces. For example, whereas a news editor would cover an air disaster, a features editor might commission a background piece on air safety or themselves research a piece on first-aid training for airline staff.

When contacting journalists, keep a note of their:

Name

Address

Phone number

Fax number

Email

Pager

Special interests

Days off

Deadline days (when *not* to contact them!)

For all the names you note down, check the spelling and write down the address to which material should be sent (not always the same as the main switchboard address). If you have an idea that you would like to suggest to one journalist in particular, you can try ringing up to talk, but many prefer to see first a written outline of what you have to suggest, sent as a fax or email. Ask if they have a personal fax number (if it goes to the general office one it may never reach them) and mark what you send 'urgent', and for their personal attention. If the person you want to speak to is not available, and someone offers to take your name and telephone number, never assume that the call will be returned.

Think about the mechanics of how you will send information to these contacts. If you are to use the names again, load them onto a database program on a computer as a mailing list, with a copy printed out on cards so you can update them when you speak in future.

> Be sure to include the local media rather than just concentrating on the nationals.

Once you have made contact, make notes about what kind of ideas they have responded to in the past (both your own and other people's), when their days off are, and when the press/air day is. The day before the press day is a good time to contact them with last-minute filler ideas; the day afterwards they will probably take off—for example, Sunday newspaper journalists seldom work on Mondays. Shortly after that is the best time to propose ideas that need thinking about in more detail such as possible future features.

Make notes on these preferences as soon as you come off the phone—after a few calls one voice will start to merge into another and you won't remember who said what. Keep a very particular note of the spelling of their name, what they like to be called (*Ms/Mrs/Miss* is particularly significant) and any relevant personal information—for example if they have just been on maternity leave or their partner has an interesting job. This may enable you to suggest an idea or specific angle on a story that appeals to them particularly.

Something to send

When pursuing publicity you need readily available information to send out. Firstly, this serves to make your story stand out, and secondly, the journalist will need something to refer to if they decide to write up what you had to say; you cannot rely on them remembering what you said on the telephone when you introduced the idea.

You may decide to use a press release to do this, or to write a letter. The press release is the basic communications tool of the publicity world; journalists look out for them and know what to do with them (there is guidance on how to write an effective press release in Chapter 5). For this reason you may decide to try to attract their attention in a different way, say with a large chocolate cake with a message on top or a personal letter. Whatever you send must:

■ be interesting

It must contain news that invites the reader to get involved. Boring information quickly becomes scrap paper.

■ be visually arresting

The most visually arresting thing you can send is a good photograph. Most media get many fewer good photographs than they would like, and too many of lines of people standing holding drinks. If your picture is imaginative, arresting, and colourful it may get used. Ensure it has a relevant caption on the back, listing in particular key names involved, the event/cause being promoted, and a simple storyline or quotation. Effective captions can end up being used whole.

For example, instead of:

> A very successful joint school fete was held by St Paul's and Alexandra Schools on Saturday.

Example

Consider being more specific:

> Over 4,000 people attended the St Paul's and Alexandra Schools Fete on Saturday, making it this year's best-attended school fete in Kingston. 'Holding a joint event means we can make it a really good one. It's exhausting but fun—and raises very valuable money for the schools. We are very grateful to the hardworking Parent–Staff Associations for all their efforts,' said the head-teachers, Miss Titterton and Mrs Ryder.

Example

You can make your text interesting by using bold and underlining (in limited measures) clever use of space (dense text is offputting; it is the space around it that draws the eye). Another effective technique is to print on coloured paper.

■ be immediate in its impact

Few press releases get used whole, if they are featured they will usually get cut from the bottom upwards.

What you send should have immediate impact, from the headline onwards. Very little of the information sent to journalists gets used whole; if it is used it will usually get cut from the bottom upwards. Journalists get hundreds of press releases every day and their attention tends to decline as the sheet goes on. For both these reasons it is vital that you start off with the main story and then work back through supporting detail in the paragraphs that follow.

■ start with a good headline

This serves to draw the eye. It does not need to be a summary of the story that follows; rather, it serves to whet the appetite for what follows.

Tip

Press releases must be:

Colourful

Imaginative

Easy to read

Not too long

■ be grammatically correct

You are writing to journalists whose stock in trade is the English language. Be very sure, therefore, that the grammar and spelling are right.

■ be easy to respond to

Suggest what you want your recipient to do as a result of receiving your information—are you inviting them to an event, to interview you or a celebrity who will promote your cause, or offering a chance to take interesting photographs (often called a 'photo-opportunity')? The example opposite offering the authors for 'interview and cocktails' is very stylish. What is more, it was printed on pink paper, which really made it stand out.

Ensure you tell the recipient how to get in touch if they want to know more. This is most often done by printing the name of the person who is sending the release and the numbers on

The *Party Blonde*

and other Social Stereotypes from the Telegraph magazine

VICTORIA MATHER ◆ SUE MACARTNEY-SNAPE

Foreword by Nicky Haslam

'Phew! What a relief. Obviously Victoria and Sue are keeping "The Ageing Sports Presenter" up their haute couture sleeves for the moment. Those who are included have once again been drawn and quartered with customary brilliance." **Desmond Lynam**

You'll recognize them immediately. You've come across them yourself or seen them in the papers: Andrew and Leonora, the smug couple, with their helicopter and their housekeeper and their brilliantly successful children Nicholas and Flora; steely American businessman Crawford Nemesis III, sent from New York to restructure Worldcorp's London office and given to lecturing his fellow dinner guests on the importance of competitive recreation. And of course, Tiffany Zeitgeist, the party blonde, who sprang to fame by wearing a fake-fur thong at a film première and who now has a weekly tabloid column which she dictates on her mobile. In this cathartic new collection of deliciously detailed social sketches, Victoria Mather and Sue Macartney Snape have English society, from top to bottom, off to a T. Perfect for the loo or the guest-room. Or slip it into your pocket to read under the table as Crawford drones boringly on.

Victoria Mather is a journalist, broadcaster, film critic and Pekinese lover. She writes regularly for *The Daily Telegraph*, is the travel editor of *Tatler* and appears on Ned Sherrin's award-wining *Loose Ends*. In her dreams she is forever by the pool of the Hotel Bel-Air in Los Angeles, wearing diamonds.

Sue Macartney-Snape's paintings of English social life are widely collected, she has had several sell-out exhibitions of her work and has been acclaimed as the Wodehouse of Art. She was born in Tanganyika, educated in Australia and now lives in London. Her first book, with text written by Jilly Cooper, was *Araminta's Wedding*.

Published: 9th November 2000   Price: £9.99

Victoria and Sue are available for interview and cocktails
*For further information please contact Stephanie Allen on tel: 020 7493 4361,
fax: 020 7499 1792, email: s.allen@johnmurrays.co.uk
John Murray Publishers, 50 Albemarle Street, London W1S 4BD*

which they can be reached at the bottom of the page. Many PR firms work on projects in teams of two or three so that there is always someone available to help. A voicemail facility that gets regularly checked is better than allowing a phone to ring and ring if you cannot be there in person. I am always heartened if a voicemail message gives the (right) date, the recipient's rough whereabouts (I am in/not in today), and the information that calls *will* be returned.

Do!

make clear what you expect of people.

Don't!

forget to include your contact details.

Put the telephone, fax, and email numbers in large bold type and double-check that they are correct. Local papers will often reproduce your telephone number for public enquiries at the end of a piece, so if you have provided an incorrect number then both the recipient of unwanted calls and the paper will be very angry. And of course in the process you will have missed out on lots of prospective customers.

If you are sending out a press release on standard organizational paper, or are writing a letter, either omit the general switchboard number at the top or change it to match the one on which you want to receive related calls. Responders will ring whichever they see first, and you want to ensure calls come back to the right number. A small picture of a phone or fax next to the relevant numbers is a very helpful.

Suggest what you want your recipient to do as a result of receiving your press release.

One final point. Give a copy of your information sheet to all those who might answer your phone, or might receive calls in connection with your information that come through on the *wrong* number. It does happen that journalists remember a story and the organization involved, but lose the relating piece of paper. They then look up the organization's general phone number and ring up someone who knows nothing about the story. Another lost opportunity.

Following up and keeping the momentum going

A difficult thing to reconcile is that most journalists hate being chased and yet they rely on the information you send in. Here is some advice on how to follow up the press releases you send out.

- If you have made a special pitch to a specific journalist, follow it up. Leave them enough time to consider your proposal but not so long they forget about it. Ask how far ahead they usually plan for each issue—this gives you an idea of the 'lead time' they need. Don't keep chasing ideas they have said no to, unless you have important new information that puts your proposal in a fascinating, or highly topical, new light.

> A 'lead time' is the time that needs to be built into a schedule for producing and printing the material.

- For a general press release you can ring your main contacts a few days after your press release mailing has gone out. But be prepared for them to say they have either lost or not received what you sent and be ready to send another, immediately, with a handwritten compliments slip.

- Get to know the names of the *other* people on the desk— don't always insist on speaking to the main correspondent.

If you feed stories to the deputy (or someone else on the desk), you will find it easier to get through, and at the same time acquire the ear of someone who can feed stories to the key person more effectively than you can yourself. What is more, in future you will have someone who *will* take your calls, when they rise to the main position themselves one day.

Think about a strategy for future press relations. What other ideas can you think of that might produce column inches and sustain your media profile? Such opportunities might include;

- long-running features in the media (e.g. Radio 4's *Desert Island Discs* or *The Sunday Times's* 'A Life in the Day of…');

Don't!

become a 'rent-a-quote', someone who is quoted too often to be credible and hence builds up 'media resistance'.

■ a regular column for a special-interest magazine;

■ a prize or fellowship for students in your field of business practice;

■ writing letters to the national press;

■ providing the occasional juicy quotation as an expert or 'media personality'.

Newsletters

What is a newsletter?

A newsletter is a regular means of communication between an organization and its market, whether they are supporters or customers.

Usually informal in tone, the format may vary (for example print or email), but the intention behind a newsletter is almost always the same—to build a long-term relationship between the parties.

The advantages and disadvantages of a newsletter

The advantage of an effective newsletter is that it is a relatively inexpensive, and yet often very effective, means of communicating. Carefully produced, with the needs and interests of those being contacted in mind, a newsletter can vary the usual pace of information delivery and promote dialogue, involvement, and loyalty.

The disadvantages are primarily organizational ones. A newsletter will not run itself. It needs a central force at the helm—whether an individual or a small group of people—who decide what goes in and what does not, on exactly the same basis as editors working on national newspapers. A badly put-together newsletter can create an instantaneously negative effect, making the organization sending it look out of touch, insensitive, or simply inappropriate.

CONTENTS

Newsletters

Pros:

Cheap to produce

Very effective

Sparks interest

Cons:

Needs lots of organization time

Must be effectively produced, with recipients' priorities in mind

A newsletter will not run itself

A very useful starting point for producing a newsletter is to think about it as a vehicle for the exchange of information. An effective newsletter is a conversation rather than a speech.

The exchange of information

An effective newsletter fosters a sense of community.

This is an important concept to grasp now. An effective newsletter boosts communication by creating and fostering a sense of community, making those who receive it feel that they are part of something that is worth belonging to or keeping in touch with. For example, this can be done by:

■ Encouraging your target readers to tell you about what they are up to so you can pass it on to the wider community of all those possibly interested. This is motivating while at the same time providing useful publicity.

■ Telling readers about innovations you have in development before the market as a whole is told of them.

■ Offering privileged access to new developments/benefits in kind/special rates for your existing services as a reward for their loyalty to you.

■ Telling them of world or industry events that affect your mutual areas of concern which they may not otherwise hear of.

- Providing practical examples of topics of current concern. This often works well on an informal basis, as an 'overheard' column. For example, teachers might be interested in relevant comments, jokes and apocryphal tales from both the playground and staffroom.

  'PSE is when you sit in a circle and talk about things you don't really understand.' Jack, aged 7*

* Note
PSE = Personal and Social Education

- Providing a vehicle for recipients to make announcements or advertise their own needs.

- Offering practical guidance on how to run a business, perhaps from the standpoint of the sender's expertise or overview of the market.

- Organizing competitions and promotions of possible interest to the reader.

- Providing a mechanism for the passing on of relevant gossip (new arrivals at a company, promotions, who has had a baby and so on).

What kind of information to include

The key to producing an effective newsletter is providing information that the market finds interesting and useful. Often, this can be the last thing on the producer's mind.

When asked to produce a newsletter, the most natural reaction is to talk about the organization in question: what is happening, what successes have occurred. It is worth bearing in mind however, that the market is likely to be far more interested in their own needs and problems than your achievements.

> An effective newsletter is a conversation rather than a speech.

It follows that new products should be described from the customer's point of view: for example, the needs that they help overcome or the general trends they anticipate. An illustration of this particular point is found in many of the personal newsletters produced by families at Christmas. Sustained boasts are seldom interesting, and can be ridiculous.

On the other hand, a more general chat about mutually interesting subjects, or the mentioning of things that did not go as planned, can be both fascinating and endearing.

As an example of good practice, the newsletter opposite from a Kent hotel is remarkably effective in both reminding previous customers to come again and prompting recommendations. Handwritten, the letter feels extremely personal, and yet is sent to a large mailing list.

As an example of bad practice, here is an extract from a newsletter from a local council, sent to every house in a London borough just before Christmas.

> *'Good conversation is as stimulating as black coffee, and just as hard to sleep after.'*
>
> Anne Morrow Lindbergh

Refuse Collection

Over the Christmas/New Year period the Council expect there to be serious problems in the disposal of the household waste collected by your refuse collectors.

In these circumstances there will be no normal refuse collections during the period from Saturday 25th December to Saturday 1st January inclusive.

To compensate for this, attached to this leaflet are three black plastic refuse sacks to store excess refuse over the Christmas/New Year period.

> The market is far more interested in its own needs and problems than your achievements.

The message above could have been presented as a good news story had the writer thought about it from the recipient's point of view rather than the council's. Christmas is a holiday period for everyone (refuse collectors included) and also produces huge amount of rubbish, and the decision to circulate bags to store the excess was imaginative. Unfortunately, rather than scooping credit for this decision, the writer chose to start the

ROMNEY BAY HOUSE

Dear Guests,

We are now almost through year 2000 and after all the hype of the Millennium this terrible wet autumn and a very dull (not many blue skies) summer, it all seems a bit of a damp squib. The New Year at Romney Bay House was very successful, not manic but I hope restful with some fun for the eve. Just at midnight we had organised some fireworks, which none of the guests knew about, everybody went onto the terrace as it was not cold, so it gave the evening a special feel.

I am happy to say we have had a very busy year, and as always it is lovely to welcome back so many of you and also to meet new guests.

As many of you will know I do have to have "no cooking" nights to enable me to continue. I do know this is not always acceptable but it is the only way at the present time and I do hope you will bear with me.

Helmut has not had a good year with jokes (thank goodness!!) We did have quite a long photo shoot from the Mail on Saturday and of course he loved that.

The cats and Lewis are very well and I hope all of you who took Lewis for a walk have now recovered.

Once again we have our popular Winter Breaks — mid-week November to March — if you need any information please phone for details.

We round off by saying, and we do mean it, we sincerely strive to keep Romney Bay House as relaxing, intimate and personal as it has always been. We are so happy on the feed back that you like and appreciate the team we have built.

May we wish you a very healthy, happy and prosperous New Year — we look forward to seeing you again.

Jennifer & Helmut

Coast Road, Littlestone
New Romney, Kent, TN28 8QY
Telephone: (01797) 364747
Fax: (01797) 367156
JENNIFER & HELMUT GÖRLICH

See Part B,
Producing a
newsletter, page 86.

letter by describing the problem and the thinking process it led
to. The consumer is far more interested in the solution.

There is a useful checklist in Part B on where to start when you
have no inspiration.

Setting up a newsletter

Why do you want a newsletter?

*'No man would
listen to you if
he didn't know
it was his
turn next.'*

Ed Howe

Are you trying to promote a completely new business or
to prevent your market from growing tired with a service or
organization they have used for many years? Are you writing to
support an existing understanding or to change perceptions?
The most appropriate style and design formats for newsletters
to meet these various situations will be very different.

For example, if you are promoting a new business you will
probably want to convey a sense of permanence: customers
need to be reassured that employing your services will not be
commercially risky. On the other hand, when writing to clients
of a long-established venture, your approach may be different.
As well as reassuring them that you continue to meet their
needs, you may wish to adopt a more human face, to stop the
customer getting bored with the service on offer.

Who is going to run this project?

A newsletter needs a focal point, an organizer or organizing
group who cares about it. They must understand why the
newsletter is being created and have very good contacts both
inside and outside the organization to pull in information and
stories that will be of interest. The person responsible also
needs to think through:

Watch out!
Beware of sending
more information
than your market
either wants
or needs.

■ How often do those you are writing to want to hear from
you? Is this compatible with your organization's commitment to the project? Beware of sending more information
than your market either wants or needs; they will start to
devalue what you send.

- What do you want recipients to do after receiving it? If you want them to circulate it, provide the relevant instruction, or perhaps a blank box under the heading 'Please circulate to' on the front cover for them to fill in. If you want them to keep it, suggest why in the copy ('This series of newsletters will form an indispensable guide to current trends in the industry') and think about sending some means of storage (a binder or folder).

- Do you want your audience to contribute? If you want to promote feedback you need to think about how you will prompt and orchestrate it. For example, if you want readers to submit letters you need to make that clear and provide details of where and whom they should write to. Newsletters can be a useful vehicle for promotions and competitions that prompt a reply or feedback.

- What about the list of contacts to which this newsletter is to be sent? Be rigorous in keeping your records up to date and try to ensure that no one is sent more than one copy. It can completely defeat the message of your newsletter if your circulation is seen to be inefficient!

Who are you writing to?

As with any form of marketing communication, the most important consideration is your audience. So:

- What kind of people are you talking to?

- What job title/responsibilities/interests do they have?

- In what circumstances are they likely to be reading what you send (how much time do they have)?

- How many of them are there?

- How is it most convenient for them to receive your information? By post? By fax? By email?

5 Newsletters

When planning a newsletter, it is a really good idea to try to get hold of some samples. Try to secure a variety, anything from the parish newsletter of a church to corporate communications to shareholders. If you are able to get hold of examples from your competitors, or those who communicate with the same people, so much the better. Remember that your competitors are a much wider group than just those who sell related products. A restaurant may compete with a gym and a hotel for the same 'personal spend'.

When looking for information to include in a newsletter, look more widely than just the obvious personal milestones: promotions, births, marriages, retirements and deaths will only occupy a small percentage of the workforce at any one time. Other personal and professional milestones could be featured, to make the newsletter more inclusive. Examples include:

- Has anyone completed an Open University degree or an evening class 'A' level?

- Who has been somewhere (whether on business or pleasure) that would be interesting for other staff members to read about?

- Is anyone appearing in an event that others could attend or get involved in: perhaps a concert, play, or swimming gala?

When it comes to company information, think about details that may not be available to everyone but which others can take pride in or simply enjoy. For example:

- What are the fastest-selling products at the moment and is there any anecdotal evidence as to why? Who is the most satisfied customer and have they said anything quotable?

- What about the opposite? Has anyone returned a product with a particularly ingenious or outrageous excuse?

What silly questions has the receptionist been asked recently? This is usually a great fund of interesting stories. I talked to the lady who runs the enquiries desk in a bookshop recently. In the previous two weeks she had been asked if the organization sold both seeds and knitting wool.

- Who else can you get to contribute to your newsletter: your suppliers, customers, friends? A third-party view can confirm an impression or pass on the information you wish to put over, but at the same time be more readily believed by your readers.

- Can you provide a 'shallow end' for readers to get started— perhaps a quiz, crossword, competition, gossip column, or cartoon which engages the recipient and encourages them to read the rest of the publication?

What should it look like?

An important stage in the creation of a newsletter is to think about how your market would like to receive your information. Print or email? What impression do you want to create: formal or informal? It is said that 90 per cent of a first impression is visual, so thinking about the style and presentation method of your newsletter is very important.

- Think about the illustrations available to divide up your text. Pay particular attention to photographs; these should be representative of the image you seek to pass on. As the photographs are likely to be the first things that get looked at, they all need an interesting caption.

'Shallow-end' hooks could include:

quizzes

crosswords

word games

competitions

gossip columns

horoscopes

cartoons

recipes

Thinking about style and presentation is very important.

■ Printing colours and layout. Should it look lavish or cheaply produced? A costly format would be inappropriate if you are raising money for a charity; probably just right if you are promoting something that is very expensive and that confers status with purchase.

See Part B, Producing a newsletter.

■ Divide up the text so it looks inviting to read rather than hard work. All articles need interesting headings and sub-headings to draw the reader in and allow them to 'skip' read. If in the process they gain the gist of a story that interests them, they may return and read the whole piece.

How long do you need to allow for production?

Work backwards from the date your material needs to be with your market, and produce a formal schedule which you circulate to everyone involved. Some newsletters will be more time-sensitive than others. For example, it would be folly to mail schools during the summer holidays (there is no one there), but academics teaching at universities may respond better at this time, when there are no students around to be taught.

Allowing too much time can be a drag on efficiency: it gives everyone the chance to change their mind. And whilst everyone responds to the occasional crisis, and producing a newsletter quickly can be very satisfying, regularly allowing too little time is not a good idea.

Watch out!
- for obvious clashes of interest, e.g. amongst colleagues and freelancers
- for availability of checkers to avoid last-minute delays.

Be clear about whom you are relying on and watch out for any obvious clashes of interest, such as other colleagues within your organization who are also relying on the same freelance designer. Watch out, too, for who needs to check your work and at what stage, in order to avoid last-minute hold ups. Check the diaries of key figures, so you don't pass them a key proof just as they leave for three weeks in South America.

Case studies of three different newsletters in action

Example

List broker Mardev produces a monthly newsletter for its publishing clients called *Publishers Direct*.

has examples of successful partnerships, including the Open Learning Foundation (OLF) and The Open Learning Company (OLC).

The successes of such groupings are characterised by two features – to which publishers can identify and respond. Successes in core markets inspire expansion into others, notably internationally and lifelong

Neil Morley

New UK Qualifications to Move Beyond Prototypes

The academic year beginning September 2001 will see the introduction of up to 20 new prototype degree courses under the auspices of what the UK Government describes proudly as a 'new qualification for a new century' – the Foundation Degree. The prototype courses will last two years. 56 HEIs are bidding to be involved.

Publishers may feel tempted to view any such new government initiative as equivalent to the historical fuss created by NVQs and GNVQs. The actual publishing opportunity may be limited in value. It may be best taken when students and institutions have had a chance to shape it around their own requirements – and, most importantly, employers have had their say about its effectiveness and contribution. There is nothing to suggest that employers favour differentiation at this level.

The marketing opportunity may be more immediate. Institutions are predicting some overlap with their HNC and HND intakes, with numbers of entrants growing overall, albeit in a more volatile

and crowded market-place. Add this prospect to the thought that a number of university aspirants may actually favour this route into higher education, and the cohort begins to look more interesting.

Working against its impact on your publishing markets are two factors. Foundation courses at any level are characterised by their need to appeal to a wide variety of entrants. As a result, they will be designed to be diverse, modular and multi-disciplinary. In past issues, Publishers Direct has argued that these factors need not deter academic and professional publishers; any market expansion should be considered as a 'good thing' although fragmentation can prove challenging to manage. By the time numbers of seats on particular Foundation courses and sub-courses are known however, the quantities of students in any market-defined area may begin to look unsustainable for a meaningful sales programme – and certainly for a publishing one. Lower status qualifications are hampered also by under-recruitment and high dropout rates.

Secondly, Foundation Degree courses are already being criticised publicly about the ways in which they will encourage students to test (without guidance) either their own suitability for higher education or the validity of the courses to actual personal aspirations.

An environment of 'testing' is not good for a commitment to book buying. Testing suggests a temporary status and a course of action that has value only as a preliminary to something else; indeed, the universities may feel tempted to sell foundation degrees that way. The seriousness of the Foundation Degree may become questionable in the minds of students and in the cultures of the HEIs themselves. If this is so, then there will be serious limitations to

commitments to investing in resources and support.

Neil Morley

Direct Mail – Hints and Tips

When I am teaching courses on direct marketing I often start the section on mailshots by asking delegates what usually goes into one. I give them the hint that there are invariably four things.

The reaction is almost always the same. Everyone remembers the letter, the response device and the leaflet. But then they draw a blank; no one can think what the fourth thing is.

To put you out of your misery, I'll tell you now. It's so obvious it gets taken for granted – it's the outer envelope.

The outer envelope gets forgotten about because it's boring; no one gets the same kick out of writing an envelope message as preparing the brochure or order form. But forgetting about it, rather than treating it as an integral part of the mailing is usually a mistake. Here are a few tips for making yours work harder.

● **Treat the envelope as part of the mailing**

Think about it along with the other items rather than at the last minute. That way it will be part of the mailshot, working towards the same objective, rather than an underused addition.

● **Consider the quality**

Envelopes come in a wide variety of standards but even if your budget is very tight, don't assume that quality does not matter. 'Cheap and cheerful' is not necessarily to your advantage. Think about what is going inside (the number of items and their combined weight) and whether a cheap envelope will stand up to

Publishers Direct was started two years ago to build relationships with customers and prospects on a regular, long-term basis. It is effective at a number of levels.

■ The newsletter underpins the company's market positioning of adviser, as opposed to purely service provider.

■ It helps Mardev demonstrate that they both understand what drives their customers' businesses and are in a position to offer practical 'how to' marketing advice.

■ On a tactical level it enables them to provide detailed information on new products and services, in some depth but in an informal context. If they were to contact each of their customers individually on the telephone, it is unlikely they would be able to take as much of their time.

■ Mardev's customers are involved in direct marketing. They have noticed that their publishing clients are relatively unsophisticated in marketing terms, in comparison with other business sectors they deal with. This offers the opportunity to share a discussion of wider trends in direct marketing that will affect publishers before long, and at the same time provide a degree of 'hand-holding' to all involved.

Although the project is managed in-house, Mardev use a range of contributing experts which keeps the investment in time manageable.

Example

Sandwich shop chain Pret A Manger has a variety of different methods of communicating with both staff and customers. There is an email every twenty-four hours to all shop managers providing the information they need for that day. Every piece of packaging that customers pick up—from napkins to carrier bags—bears the company telephone number and website address; these numbers lead to real people who do answer the phone, and there is a very positive attitude to customer feedback and suggestions.

A regular newsletter for all staff aims to give a sense of the wider organization they are working for. The editor of this newsletter has to bear a number of considerations in mind:

Well, I had to go and open my big mouth, didn't I?

When I said in last month's 'Pret Star', "can we try and beat last Christmas's record of 322 messages?", no way did I ever expect to end up with 480 of the damn things! That truly is amazing, it means that about 1 in every 4 people who work for Pret have received or sent a message this issue. I bet there aren't many staff magazines that have that level of interaction with their readers!

Thanks to Line and especially David for helping out with all the typing up. If it wasn't for those two, there's no way we'd have got this issue out to you for today. (And sorry if your name's been spelt wrong or we haven't quite got your message right – but some of you have got truly terrible handwriting:-)

I was even sent one message via email from Italy! Francesca, who worked in West One for a year until six months ago, wanted to say hi to all the good friends she left behind when she went back home. It just goes to show that this company has some pretty damn unforgettable people working for it, and that there's a good chance that during your time working for Pret, you'll meet people who are destined to become your life-long friends.

This year I've had my ups and downs, the same as everybody else. But there's a gang of people who've kept me going, and that's the Pretarazzi. So I want to dedicate this issue to them – the team past and present – and wish them in particular a very very very Merry Christmas. Enjoy your break, guys, 'cos I'm gonna work you damn hard in the New Year! Thanks to Titus and Damian for providing a bit of stability when everything else seemed to be changing. And special thanks also to Marc and Caroline who do so much behind-the-scenes to keep the "Star" fresh and funky; ie. the sort of magazine you want to send 500 messages to!

See you all in 2001, when our first issue will be packed with highlights from the Christmas Party.

Love
Nigel

STAR PERFORMERS

CONGRADULATIONS!

...to everyone who graduated during November

WEST LONDON
Team Leader:
Moh (Kensington)
TM-Stars: Mauricio,
Thomas (Kings Road),
Juan, Luiza, Jachen,
Carla, Abdelghani,
Bidur, Simon, Alan
(Earls Court).

AROUND TCR
Team Leaders:
Francesco (Euston
Tower); Hope (St
Martins Lane)
Trainers: Luca
(Camden); Lorena
(New Oxford St);
Chiara (122HH);
Mazie (100TCR)
TM-Stars: Saija (New
Oxford St); Catarina,
Celia, Frida, Farid,
Stef (18 Martins Lane)

FLEET & HOLBORN
Team Leaders: Raquel
(74 Fleet St); Jean
(319 HH); Karim
(New Bridge St);
Vania (135 Strand)
Trainers: Celine
(Stamford St);
TM-Stars: Sonia
(Holborn Viaduct);
Anna (Ludgate Hill);
Djakily (Stamford St)
Barista: Ahmed
(240 HH)

SOUTH OXFORD ST
Team Leaders:
Adam (Carnaby St);
Cherif (West One)
Trainers: Johanna
(Soho); Lone, Noella
(West One)
TM-Stars: Ellal,
Giovanna, Mahmoud,
Tina, Vannessa, Eric,
Fabio (West One);

Moses (Carnaby St)

**PICCADILLY, STRAND
& SOUTH**
Baristas: Kastriot
(421 Strand), Daol
(Kingsgate)

CITY
Team Leader: Dominic
(Goswell Road)
Trainer: Christophe
(Cheapside)
TM-Stars: Kamarta
(Bow Lane); Kapela,
Adewale (138 Cannon
St); Stephanie (Goswell
Road); Ahmet (Grays
Inn Rd); Klaude,
Adriane, Tundak,
Richmond (Turnmill
St)
Barista: Vincent
(Theobalds Road)

HEART OF THE CITY
Trainers: Nassila
(Whitecross Place);
Joao (Winchester
House)
TM-Stars: Miriam (140
Bishopsgate); Eric,
Timothy (Broadgate);
Baristas: Manuel (140
Bishopsgate); Michael
(St Mary Axe)

**THAMES & SOUTH
LONDON**
Barista: Farida
(Canary Wharf)

UK SOUTH
Team Leader: Sharon
(Cambridge)
Barista: Anna
(Folkestone)

UK MIDLANDS
TM-Stars: Sandra,
Lynda, Martin (Milton

Keynes); Mark
(Oxford)
Barista: Mark
(Nottingham 2)

UK NORTH
Team Leaders:
Jo (Meadowhall);
Sarah (York)
Trainers: Sandra
(Rothwell St); Lee,
Matts (Leeds);
Caroline
(Meadowhall); Marc
(Spring Gardens);
TM-Stars: Zoe, John,
Lisa (Rothwell St)
Baristas: Jackie
(Meadowhall); Maria
(Leeds)

NEW YORK
Trainers: Dan, Jose,
Monique

**...And to these
recently-graduated
MITs**
Oti Rahman (trained
in Baker St), Rachid
Anös (140
Bishopsgate), Andrew
Jones (Canary Wharf),
Ashish Mishra (52
Cannon St), Ron
Curran (28 Fleet St),
Justine Etridge
(Kensington), Annicca
Ericsson (Leather
Lane), Steven Chan
(162 Piccadilly),
Myriam Duveau
(Turnmill St), Brent
Christianson Watt (84
Piccadilly), Said
Takhaznt (421
Strand), Karim Khane
(75b Victoria), Andrew
Shanahan (West One),
and Lucy Ogley
(York).

A special well done to new Ops Manager Justine, who couldn't have done any better on her MIT exam – she got 100%! Those Kensington guys obviously give great Management training!

CHARCUTERIE
continental

THANKS TO THE ATMs FOR SUPPLYING US WITH THE MAJORITY OF THESE NAMES.

■ What appears to the customer as an informal and relaxed working environment is in fact very structured, with clear differentiation of tasks and corresponding levels of training. A public acknowledgement of commitment and success as staff progress through these programmes is important.

■ Any service industry is at the mercy of its customers, who can be rude, dishonest, and downright difficult. To offset the occasional unfortunate incident, it is enjoyable for readers to hear about celebrities who have been spotted or funny incidents that have taken place in the stores.

■ A communications strategy for an organization must involve employees.

■ The food retail market often draws staff from a group for whom English is not their first language. The layout thus has to be inviting to read and easy to understand.

■ The staff pool also includes individuals who will be passing through whilst travelling. It is important to give them a sense of the wider organization, so that they will pass the name on and at the same time boost enquiry levels and community spirit.

■ The newsletter plays an important part in creating a sense of the wider organization, offering information and gossip about what is going on in various branches.

In style, the magazine is a cross between *Time Out* and *Private Eye*. The editor of the magazine was Editor of the Year (staff publication) in the 1999 Total Publishing Press Group Media Awards. The judges commented on how well the publication reflected the feel of the organization it represented.

Email and faxed newsletters are an excellent way of providing fast and brief information to a specific market.

Example

TV International Daily is a newsletter sent daily to a (paid) subscriber base, either by email or by fax. The same organization produces the fortnightly print and electronic publication *TV*

International. The email newsletter is available on subscription, at a higher price to a much smaller market, and serves to provide subscribers with information that is:

- Current. Whereas the fortnightly publication analyses and describes trends, the email daily seeks to pass on the current stories as (or preferably just before) they break.

- Concise. Almost never more than one side of A4, although the email version can be slightly longer as there is no space limit. The lead story will seldom be more than 350 words; other items much shorter. For clients who want longer analysis or future predictions, the fortnightly publication fulfils their needs.

- Accurate. Information included is likely to be acted on straightaway, and so accuracy and reliability are of the utmost importance. It is vital that subscribers trust the organization and its sources.

```
> _____
>
> NATIONAL GEO ENTERS ARGENTINA
> Argentine cable system operator added National Geographic
> Channel on April 1, lifting the channel's Latin American sub
> count from 3 million to 4 million. Nat Geo launched in Brazil
> last year and has plans to roll out the service to most of the key
> Latin markets over the next several months.
>
> _____
>
> QVC OPENS DOORS IN JAPAN
> Shopping channel QVC launched a 24-hour service in Japan
> April 1 to 1.2 mil. cable and 2.5 mil. SkyPerfect DTH
> subscribers. QVC Japan is a 60% subsidiary of QVC along with
> local partner Mitsui., which holds 40%. The channel features 15
> hours of live programming. Liberty Media owns 42.6% of QVC.
>
> _____
```

'Facts speak louder than statistics.'

Geoffrey Streatfield (lawyer)

■ Privileged. The newsletter gives subscribers information that shows them to be in the know; an overview of the market which they can display at meetings they attend, thereby stealing a march on their competitors and, not infrequently, their own colleagues! This publication goes to senior people in the industry, or those who aspire to be so.

■ Packed. The sender aims to make best possible use of the space available. The designer's brief is to present a great deal of information in the way that the reader's eye is likely to find easiest to read. The layout of the email version is obviously dependent on the recipient's programme settings, but a standard layout on despatch helps make it easy to read— asterisks at the top of the newsletter, headlines always in capital letters, an underline at the end of the story, a return at end of each line so that the margin is consistent and not too wide.

Press releases

What is a press release?

A press release is the basic communication tool for those wanting to talk to journalists. Usually consisting of a short message (most are under one side of A4 paper, less if sent by email), it aims to convey the essence of a story in the hope of prompting coverage in the medium being approached.

Why send a press release?

Sending a press release is a bid to get coverage. It is hoped that the journalist receiving it will respond by doing one of two things:

- Decide to use the information it contains 'whole', i.e. use the wording in the press release to form an article in the medium being approached

- Decide to give the story greater prominence, either by interviewing the characters involved, commissioning a feature, or investigating the subject further.

When not to send a press release

A press release should be part of a planned media strategy; you should never send one without thinking about what you want to say, and how the media you are approaching are likely to react. As a general rule, only send a press release when there is genuine news or a real story to impart. If you use your press

CONTENTS

Only send out a press release when you have something to say.

releases to pass on boring information, or send them too regularly, those who receive them will get used to binning them on sight.

If you have a very interesting story or piece of news, rather than sending a general press release to everyone likely to be interested, your time may be better occupied making a specific pitch to a single medium; perhaps offering them a 'scoop' or access to a story before it is released to any other medium.

Understanding the recipient's environment: what are journalists like?

'Journalism. An ability to meet the challenge of filling space.'
Rebecca West

Journalists are lazy; at least work on the basis that they are. Spoonfeed them useful information. They are also incredibly busy: in offices overflowing with paper just reaching the desk can be a minor marathon. There is not the time to read all the information sent in, which is why presentation of material does matter. If you want a journalist to read what you send, make it snappy and clear.

Whilst they can even be arrogant—they know that those who contact them want coverage—still, the relationship with those who submit press releases is entirely symbiotic: they need stories as much as you need coverage. If you can harness your mutual interests together, you will both benefit.

Paula Johnson, journalist and former literary editor of The Mail on Sunday

'Literature is the art of writing something that will be read twice; journalism what will be grasped at once.'
Cyril Connolly

What can we extract from this? Journalists' working conditions are frenetic. The phone rings constantly; postal deliveries bring new batches of information before the last lot has even been digested. The inbox on their computer records emails galore demanding their attention.

This means that the information you send in the form of a press release will get only the most cursory of glances, and if it is not clear what is being offered, and why it is interesting, few will have the time to delve any further.

What the journalist looks for immediately

■ The first paragraph is very important: it needs to include the 'who, what, where, why, and when'. All the basics of the story must be there.

■ The remaining paragraphs need to tease out issues of interest that can either bulk out a story if reproduced whole or form the basis of a feature, should they decide to investigate further.

'Journalists are lazy; at least work on the assumption that they are.'

■ The press release must be clearly referenced: the journalist must know who it is from and how to get in touch with the person who sent it. The numbers you quote (telephone, email, and fax) must be right to avoid wasting everyone's time.

■ Your text must be grammatically correct. Remember that with a press release you are approaching journalists, who are wordsmiths. They write for media that other people will read or consult, and therefore their language must be precise. Yours should be the same.

> If I see a misplaced apostrophe in a press release, or other serious grammatical lapse, I bin it—unless the story looks to be very, very interesting.
>
> Ged Scott, sports feature writer, Birmingham Post

■ The press release must be laid out in a way that makes it easy to read and absorb. Dense copy is seldom eye-catching.

■ Spell their name correctly. Address the current correspondent rather than their predecessor.

The importance of a story

A story is vital to any press release, because it is part of your bargain with the journalist.

'If names are not correct, language will not be in accordance with the truth of things.'
Confucius

Let's take the newspaper journalist as an example (although the same principles apply to journalists working in any medium of communications, from magazines to television studios). It is important to understand that if the journalist does act on your press release, and write about the proposition you have suggested, they will be giving you space in their newspaper for nothing. What is more, they can put a price on the space they give you, and the advertising sales team have a rate card to prove it. Even more important, if your message appears as part of the main paper rather than an advertising feature, it will be more believable to the market, far more so than advertising copy, which is assumed to be partisan. So in addition to costing you nothing, your message becomes more believable.

What does the journalist want in return? A story. A tale that will interest their readers and prompt them to carry on buying the paper. Even better if it is a story 'with legs', or one that will keep running, prompting letters and responses and attracting news in its own right.

Newspapers want stories because they help keep their readership loyal

'Have you noticed that life, real honest-to-goodness life, with murders and catastrophes and fabulous inheritances, happens almost exclusively in the newspapers?'

Jean Anouilh

Newspapers offer their readers a mixture of fact and opinion. Reporters on the ground, or talking to those on the ground, try to establish the truth about what is going on for the news pages. Then feature writers interpret it and add their own opinion. But the bottom line is that the viewpoint taken by the paper will serve to reinforce the beliefs and attitudes of the readership, and keep them loyal to the paper. There will be a slightly different viewpoint taken in every paper, depending on the views of the market they believe they are talking to.

It follows that information presented to journalists in a manner sympathetic to the readership they write for stands a much better chance of being used than a 'one size fits all' approach. So if a story is important to you, tailor what you write in the press release for the medium you are targeting.

What is a story?

Story-telling is one of mankind's oldest traditions. Long before people could read or write, stories were passed down by telling out loud. The essence of a good story is that it is memorable, that it resonates with those to whom it is addressed, and that they in turn want to pass it on.

> The essence of a good story is that it is memorable.

A good story often starts with an individual, with whose experiences the listener can identify and sympathize. It is much easier to identify with the problems or struggles of one individual than with a mass of people, and to grasp a broader issue at the same time. Ancient stories told of the heroic struggles of one individual (e.g. Icelandic sagas, Virgil's *Aeneid*, and Homer's *Odyssey*).

The same principle holds good for influencing journalists today: to illustrate a point in general, home in on a sympathetic example and tell their story. Journalists call this 'an angle' (e.g. 'What's your angle?') but the principle is the same. If your story is a single issue, such as the need for a bypass around a village centred on a very busy road, then your best plan may be to highlight the family of someone hurt. Along similar lines, you can make a story out of the launch of a new product by:

Journalese

'what's your angle?'

'this story has legs'

'this is one to run with'

'does it hit you?'

- Talking about how the need for the product came to light, and about one person's experiences that illustrate the problem that the product is designed to solve.

 Don't!
misspell any names that you mention. Nothing annoys people more.

- Talking about how the product came to be produced—the administrative and logistical difficulties that were overcome and the human factors that were involved. For example, instead of citing late-night working for everyone involved, be specific—here's why one father hasn't seen his children whilst they were awake all week.

- Disproving previously held theories and popular wisdom. For example, it was said that this product was unaffordable; well, here's one family who can now enjoy it.

So looking at the information at your disposal, and extracting the story therein, is the main skill when trying to write a press release. Here is an example in practice. The following text is from a press release to advertise a forthcoming new book, based on the long-running Radio 4 series *Gardeners' Question Time*.

> Gardeners' Question Time is quite simply a gardening institution. For over 50 years 'the team' has been Britain's voice of expert advice and common sense on all things gardening. Beautifully produced and illustrated, this book is the ultimate, most invaluable source of gardening information available.
>
> ● Radio 4's Gardeners' Question Time has been the top radio show for over 50 years.
>
> ● It attracts 1.3 million listeners each week.
>
> ● Research shows that there are just 350 questions or variants of questions which cover 95% of all those asked: this book is a compilation of these questions and answers.
>
> ● The book is divided into five informative sections: Trees, Shrubs and Herbaceous (John Cushnie), Pests and Diseases (Pippa Greenwood), Fruit and Vegetables (Bob Flowerdew), Garden Design (Bunny Guinness) and House Plants (Anne Swithinbank).
>
> ● Where appropriate, the answers incorporate specialist information, such as organic alternatives from Bob Flowerdew, pest treatment from Pippa Greenwood and design tips from Bunny Guinness.
>
> ● Gardeners' Question Time: All Your Gardening Problems Solved is illustrated with 90 black and white line drawings to show diseases and techniques and over 70 full colour photographs.
>
> ● There is a comprehensive cross-reference index.

This press release features a variety of different kinds of information, but whereas this might be helpful on a promotional leaflet, there are perhaps too many themes for an effective press release. Several of the above points could be developed into a single story for the journalist, for example:

■ Although the programme has been going for over 50 years, only 350 questions were ever asked.

■ The number of listeners is interesting, and would make a good comparison with television figures for well-known programmes. Many people assume television is the modern medium of communication, and an effective case for radio can be made through this programme.

■ The book effectively offers five garden experts in one, given the different specialities involved. So given the current interest in home improvement programmes, the book could effectively be presented as '*Ground Force* meets Plant *ER*'.

Bullet points 4 and 5 are virtually the same, point 6 repeats information presented just before the bullet points and point 7 is not very interesting. Cutting down these bullet points into fewer, interesting themes would both give the release much more impact and make it easier for the journalist to use— therefore making it more likely that it will lead to coverage.

Timing

The timing of a press release needs careful consideration

The timing of a press release needs careful consideration. If you send it too long before the event you wish to publicize, you risk it getting forgotten. Send it at too short notice and the diaries of those you wish to attend may already be full.

One solution is to use a series of press releases to announce different aspects of the same event. For example, if one of your products is nominated for a major prize you could send out:

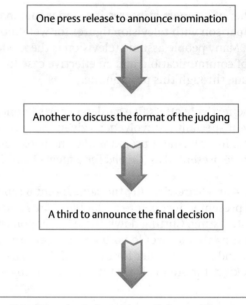

One press release to announce nomination

Another to discuss the format of the judging

A third to announce the final decision

A fourth to discuss how winning (or not) changed the entrant's life.

Alternatively, you may decide to put an embargo on your press release. This means adding a date before which the release may not be used. It should be noted that sometimes embargo dates are ignored by a specific medium in order to 'scoop' their rivals.

Design and layout for maximum effect

You will find that the more information you include in a press release, the harder it is to read. Space is essential to draw the reader's eye:

The art of typography is laying out the space around which the words will fit, not the other way around.

Derek Birdsall, Royal Designer to Industry

Hints on making the text more eye-catching:

■ Don't use too many typefaces or stylistic devices (e.g. resist using lots of different styles of bullet points).

■ Ensure paragraphs are of different lengths—it can look very box-like if every paragraph is the same extent.

■ Unless the text measure is very narrow, have a ragged right-hand margin, rather than justified text—again, the spaces created serve to draw the reader's eye.

> The more information you include in a press release, the harder it will be to read.'

■ Use illustrations to liven up your text; line drawings and cartoons work particularly well.

■ Make limited use of text emphasizers (e.g. bold, underlining, capitals) to draw attention to the parts of your message you consider particularly important.

■ Have a bold headline at the top that is interesting and contains only one theme.

■ Ensure the contact information is clearly accessible at the bottom of the page.

■ As most press releases are sent on white paper, consider printing on coloured stock to make it stand out.

The anatomy of a press release

Having talked in detail about the environment in which your press release will land, and the basics it will require, it's time to discuss a sample in detail (see following page).

MEDIA BRIEFING
24/05/2001
LEAGUE AGAINST CRUEL SPORTS

Press Office, Sparling House, 83 – 87 Union Street, London SE1 1SG
(tel) 0207 403 6155 (fax) 0207 403 4532 (press mobile) 07977 239 406 (web) www.league.uk.com

May 24, 2001

FRANK FOX JOINS ANTI-HUNTING
CAMPAIGNERS IN SITTINGBOURNE

Frank the Fox was costumed up and walking down **Sittingbourne High Street** (outside the Forum shopping centre) at **4pm on Wednesday 23rd May**. He joined local Parliamentary candidate **Derek Wyatt (Labour)** who is in favour of a ban and is seeking re-election. They gave out balloons and leaflets, and spoke to local residents.

With both Labour and Liberal Democrat parties committed to allowing MPs to finally resolve the long-running hunting debate, this election will finally decide whether hunting is to be banned or allowed to continue

League Against Cruel Sports campaigners believe that hunting of wild mammals with dogs is an immoral act of gross cruelty to animals.

John Cooper, Chairman of the League, said, "Subject to the election of sufficient pro-ban MPs at the general election, the next Government will bring an end to the hunting of deer, foxes, hare and mink."

Labour has promised "an early opportunity" to "enable Parliament to reach a conclusion on this issue" [manifesto] and to reintroduce the Hunting Bill [Tony Blair quote at manifesto press conference]. And the Liberal Democrats say that "the issue of hunting with hounds should be settled by MPs on a free vote." [manifesto]

John Cooper added, "Opinion poll after opinion poll has regularly shown a 2:1 majority in favour of a ban on hunting. This is a tremendous time for the League Against Cruel Sports which has been campaigning against hunting for 77 years."

Ends

Note for Editors: For more information, phone the League Against Cruel Sports campaigns office on 020 7403 6155 or **Dave Ward** on 07779 599 919.

League Against Cruel Sports Ltd. Registered in England as a Company. No. 2880406. Registered office 83-87 Union Street, London SE1 1SG

- **Source**: it should be instantly clear who your press release is from.

- **Date of release**, and if it is embargoed (no one may use it before the stated time).

- **Headline**: all press releases need a headline to attract attention. A headline does not need to be a perfect summary of the story that follows; rather, it serves to attract the reader's attention. For a press release aimed at a local medium, the key location must be in the headline (in this case, Sittingbourne).

- **The first paragraph is crucial**. It should contain all the basic information (the 'who, what, where, why, and when') in case the reader gets no further.

- **Additional paragraphs**: expand on themes relating to the main story. These may be used by the journalist whole if space permits/time is pressing, or form the basis of their own investigation.

- **A quotation from the organization in question or other interested parties**. This is a good idea, as it enables the journalist to make their article sound more widely researched without needing to talk to anyone else.

- **Statistics** are a great way to confirm a point. In this case, the press release quotes general opinion polls which add weight to their argument. Quoting the actual name of the poll, its date, and the specific findings it reported would carry even more weight, or quoting the number of surveys over a specific period—e.g. in the last two years fifteen separate polls have reported a consistent picture: that Britain is anti-hunting by a margin of 2:1.

- **The final paragraph**: here the sender needs to tell the journalist what to do next. In this case a photo opportunity is available and the phone numbers are clearly laid out.

'Statistics will prove anything, even the truth.'
Noel Moynihan

Actress Jean Boht lends a hand to Marie Curie

Photocall...Photocall...Photocall...

Date: **Wednesday, June 6, 2001**
Time: **11.00 am**
Venue: **Marie Curie shop, 142 High Street, New Malden, Surrey**

Actress Jean Boht will be lending a hand at the Marie Curie shop in New Malden on Wednesday (June 6) in aid of Volunteers' Week.

Jean will be joining the charity's dedicated volunteers who help out in Marie Curie Cancer Care's shop and will be calling on others to follow her example.

Volunteers' Week (June 1 to 7) aims to celebrate the tremendous work volunteers do for charities like Marie Curie throughout the year, and hopes to encourage more people to donate some of their time to help others.

Money raised in the Marie Curie shop in New Malden will help fund the 32 Marie Curie Nurses in Surrey, who care for people seriously ill with cancer and their families in the comfortable and familiar surroundings of their own homes, completely free of charge.

Ends

For further information:

Kerry French or Sue Price, Marie Curie PR Department on 020 7599 7705 or 7702

Date of issue: June 4, 2001

Here is another example of a press release, this time from Marie Curie Cancer Care.

It is very clear who this release is from, and it is also well sign-posted who the release is for.

The 'who, what, where, why and when' is very clearly demonstrated at the top of the page. It would be helpful, however, to know who the actress is. This could be done by giving the names of parts she has played, or even better by showing her photograph if she is instantly recognizable.

It would be good too to make a link between her and the charity she is supporting; is she local to New Malden or does she support Marie Curie in general?

7 Troubleshooting

'It is a good rule
in life never to
apologise. The
right sort of
people do not
want apologies
and the wrong
sort take advan-
tage of them.'

P. G. Wodehouse

Introduction

We are nearing the end of this book and I am hoping that a consistent message has been received throughout: before communicating formally with anyone you should think carefully about what you plan to say—from what impression you will create to whether or not you would be happy for your competitors to read it. Communication is too serious a matter to be dealt with casually.

This is all the more important today given the rise of the customer services culture, where consumers feel justified in actively pursuing satisfaction, if not compensation, from those they enter into trading relationships with.

So what do you do when problems do arise with your promotional materials—anything from angry letters from dissatisfied customers to a misunderstanding of your message which ends up being distorted by the press?

Why has this problem arisen?

Has there been insufficient checking of text/message? This is a difficult thing to manage. Too many sets of eyes checking a piece of copy can be a brake on creativity. The urge to fiddle with someone else's copy is irresistible, particularly if you are the manager and by amending something you fulfil the process of managing. Yet it is vital that the message sent out is consistent with the overall aims and ethos of the organization.

For example, if the publicity department of an educational publisher were to send out press releases containing serious grammatical errors, it would make the firm's claim to provide effective teaching resources laughable, and could support an entirely unhelpful news story in the media.

Dealing with letters of complaint

Ensure you reply, and promptly. If it will take you some time to investigate the problem, write a holding letter ('Thank you for bringing this matter to our attention. We will investigate and reply as soon as possible.')

Is the complaint justified? If so, you may wish to offer some form of compensation to counteract the customer's disappointment (beware of admitting liability, as this may open the gates for the litigious). If you offer your own goods, then remember that the perceived value to the customer is much greater than the actual cost to you, so a voucher for goods from your organization has a greater perceived benefit than actual cost. If you handle your complainers well they can become ambassadors for your company, and more ready to order from you in future.

Reply promptly to letters of complaint.

Avoid humour in letters answering complaints, or contemporary references that will date or sound condescending. Adopt a tone of serious concern and sweet reason.

'It is a luxury to be understood.'
Ralph Waldo Emerson

> I can well appreciate your concerns and assure you that this is absolutely not the impression we wish to give our customers.

Address the response to the person who wrote to you (not their spouse) and ensure you get the details of their name and address correct—a mistake in a letter of response will just confirm their impression of yours as a sloppy organization.

What to do when journalists get it wrong

If a newspaper or broadcast programme prints something that is not true, they are obliged to use the same medium to present a denial in the next edition. Few, however, allocate the same amount of space to the denial as to the original news piece.

What if a journalist presents the story you do not want to see featured and then comes back to you for a comment? How you respond will depend on your own inclinations. If you respond you will be continuing the debate; for this reason you may decide to say nothing and hope the story dies for lack of fuel.

The other view is that 'No comment' means no chance to put your point of view. If you do decide to take part, try to do so in a rational and unemotional manner, getting across the key messages you wish to impart rather than refuting every allegation in minute detail.

The following guidance will be useful in helping to avoid these situations arising in future.

Getting feedback on your marketing materials

You send out your press release or marketing newsletter and hear nothing back. Should you assume that everyone has read it and remembered it, or the opposite? Should you chase it up?

A focus group may give you feedback on what is routinely misunderstood

It's a very good idea to set up some sort of focus group that meets on a regular basis to provide feedback on things that may be routinely misunderstood but no one will ever tell you about. For example:

■ A primary head teacher was used to receiving 'shared mailings' from companies wishing to reach schools. This is a commonly used device where several mailers put their material in the same envelope to share costs. The head teacher in question assumed that whatever was on the top of the polythene envelope was the theme for that mailing; so if the first thing he saw was a new swimming pool brochure, he assumed the rest of the package would be similar items. In fact, absolutely the opposite is the case: the organizers of such mailings do not include materials of rival companies in the same pack.

- Is your terminology confusing to customers? Do you use words that have no meaning outside the confines of your office? Publishers routinely use words like 'softback' or 'limp' to describe books that the vast majority of the population refers to as 'paperbacks'. Beware alienating potential customers, making your organization sound like a club that they don't belong to.

Setting up a focus group

One very effective way of finding out about the impression your marketing materials make is to ask for feedback through a focus group.

The venue should be informal and appropriate in size (you will be able to create a more intimate atmosphere in a small room than a large hall) and you should provide sustenance to encourage those who attend to see the meeting as a treat rather than a burden. Most contributors enjoy the chance to take part, and the gathering always allows opinion to progress at a greater pace because one person's opinions prompt others to take the debate further. It is a good idea to send out sample marketing materials before the meeting so that those attending can have a chance to look through them, also to ask them to bring along samples of marketing materials that they think are either effective or ineffective.

Ideas for discussion at a focus group on marketing materials:

- How do you like to be contacted? Through the post, by email, in person?

'The real art of conversation is not only to say the right thing in the right place, but to leave unsaid the wrong thing at the tempting moment.'
Dorothy Nevill

A focus group is a forum for discussion, allowing members of the market the chance to report directly to you on their reactions to the communications you put out.

Keep a file of all your communications along with notes, cuttings, or copies of the response you got. You may get future inspiration from this file—ideas that work once may work again—as well as ideas of what to avoid.

■ What do you think of the overall look of the leaflets: do they invite you to read them?

■ How interesting are the headlines? Do they draw your attention?

■ What about the amount of information included—is there too little or too much?

■ Design and layout—is it appealing, easy to read? Do you like the colours? Are they easy to read? Is the text large enough to read?

■ Special offers—do they attract your attention, do you find them appealing, would it make you spend more money?

■ What about the tone of the copy—is it engaging/patronizing/just right?

■ Which organizations produce marketing information that you find motivating to read and easy to respond to?

■ Do you open your post yourself or does someone do it for you? Does what gets passed to you get filtered—i.e. not everything received is passed on? How much of your post do you open? Do you look at everything you receive, look at most of what you receive, or look carefully at the envelope before deciding whether or not to open it at all?

■ Do you pass on marketing information that you know would be of interest to someone else? Would you be willing to provide us with the names and addresses of those you send information to?

Part B: Reference section
Contents

Options for getting a message across

Paid for	Free
Space advertising	Free publicity
Direct marketing	
Promotions	
Competitions	

Advantages

You have control of the message	Costs nothing
You decide on the timing	Believable to the market
You can be sure it went out/was circulated	Can be very effective

Disadvantages

You cannot be sure it will get read	You lose control of the message
It may be disbelieved because it is *your* information	Takes a long time to organize
	You may end up with nothing

The writing process—a checklist

☐ Discuss what it is you are to write, why, and what you hope to achieve as a result.

☐ Make a list of all those who need to check your copy, keeping it as short as possible.

☐ Do the research—find out more about the topic/product/ event you are to write about, read publications read by the market, find out what else they receive, talk to members of the market if that is possible.

☐ Start thinking about your message.

☐ Make notes on your key themes.

☐ Think about the structure of what you will write.

☐ Is the planned format the most sensible way of getting the message across? Can you think of a better solution?

☐ Think.

☐ Write your copy from memory.

☐ Recheck against your notes to ensure you have included the main messages.

☐ Leave your text for several days (or at least overnight) before circulating it to those who must check it.

☐ Try to distinguish between changes that need making and those that must be discussed. Negotiate.

Dividing up your copy

Very few of those reading promotional materials will start at the beginning and work their way systematically to the end. If you have ever tried to proofread your own material you will know that this is true. Most people's reading habits are much more haphazard—they jump from item to item, waiting for their attention to be drawn.

It is important, therefore, to use devices to draw the reader in—to attract their attention to the parts of the text you consider most important. All the following are effective techniques for this. But be warned: they lose their effectiveness if over-used.

■ Headlines draw the reader in.

They do not have to be a perfect summary of the story that follows; rather, they are something to entice the reluctant reader. A good headline leads the reader into the rest of the story. Headlines work best at the top of text, in a horizontal position: if the reader has to turn the page round to read it, many won't bother.

■ Headings and sub-headings.

Dense text with no headings to signpost the reader as to content is very hard work. Ensure that both headings and sub-headings are interesting, and not too long. Questions make interesting headings. Reading all the sub-headings in a text should be a shorthand way of understanding the message.

■ Numbering paragraphs is a useful way of drawing attention to the key parts of the message:

> The enclosed brochure spells out in detail all you need to know about our new service, but there are a couple of things that I would like to draw your attention to in particular.

A numbered list of benefits followed.

■ Bullet points are useful

But there is a danger is in using too many. I find three or four is plenty. Use more and your text can look riddled with them. Many attractive styles are available (●, ■, ☞, ✳) but resist the temptation to have more than one in each promotion piece!

■ Indenting text works well for extra emphasis, and is a particularly good way of drawing attention to quotations:

> 'Show me a laundry list and I'll set it to music.' Rossini

Put copy in a box, perhaps with a pale colour or tint behind it.

■ Use outsize inverted commas (I think of them as tadpoles) to attract attention to quotations and testimonials.

66 This is superb, **99** said the Managing Director. **66** Buy it instantly. **99**

■ Make limited use of underlining, bold, italic, and capital letters (all can be very hard to read if used extensively).

■ Use illustrations, but make sure each one has an interesting caption—the captions will probably get read before the main text.

■ Reverse copy out of a solid colour. This works well for short words (*New, Free, Out Now!*) but can be very hard on the eyes for longer amounts of text.

■ Allow plenty of white space between your text. It is the space that draws the eye in to read a piece of text, not the words.

Whilst all the above are useful techniques, do not use them too often, or in too many combinations. Their positive effects are destroyed if they compete for the reader's attention and draw it away from the overall message you wish to communicate.

Checklist for producing a newsletter

Why am I writing a newsletter?

☐ What do we want to get out of it?

☐ What is the long-term commitment to the project?

☐ How often will it appear?

☐ For how long?

☐ How will it be judged a success or failure?

Who will be running this project?

☐ Do they have the resources that they need (time, budget, talent, etc.)?

Who am I writing to?

☐ What kind of people, reading in what kind of circumstances?

☐ What kind of style and tone is appropriate to this group?

☐ What initial/lasting impression do I want to make?

☐ Do I want feedback, and if so how will this be managed?

☐ Who else is writing for this market and how?

What should it look like?

☐ What is the most suitable format (e.g. print or email, number of colours, quality of images)?

☐ How much should I write?

☐ What illustrations are available?

☐ Who else can I get to contribute?

What is the schedule for production?

☐ When does the market need to have it in their hands? (Work back from this date.)

☐ Are there any critical external constraints, e.g. must be received by the end of term?

☐ Am I allowing too much time or too little?

☐ Who am I relying on?

☐ Who has to check it, and how long should I allow for this?

Checklist for writing a press release

Do I need a press release?

☐ Have I got anything interesting to say?

☐ Would an individual approach be more successful?

What story do I have to tell?

☐ Any individual tales that prove the point?

☐ Any statistics that support my case?

☐ Any third-party anecdotes/trends on the same theme?

How can I get over the story in a nutshell?

☐ The who, what, where, when, and why for the first paragraph?

☐ What headline can I use to draw the reader in?

☐ What supporting themes can I develop to sustain interest?

☐ What follow-up action can I suggest (e.g. photo opportunity or interview)?

Basic things to check before sending out a press release

☐ Is it clear who sent it?

☐ Is the contact information correct (check all numbers given)?

☐ Is it visually varied and attractive to look at?

☐ Would I read it myself if it were in my post?

Where to start when you have no inspiration

What do you do when asked to write something, and no inspiration is forthcoming?

Should you volunteer anything? Will the circulation of information you could not spontaneously produce yourself reduce your image in the recipient's eyes? Think about this seriously before you go any further.

If you still need a starting point, say for a regular slot in a house newsletter or an idea for a publicity-planning meeting, consider the following:

- Why was the organization/product/pressure group created?

- What needs does it meet that were previously unfulfilled, and how can it be provably shown that this is the case? Any individuals that can be cited will be helpful.

- What has been said about your organization recently? Any testimonials/letters/reviews?

- Are you topical? Are you following (or creating?) a trend that is being widely reported and which you can ride on the back of?

- What is the format of what you are offering? Is there anything new/exciting/convenient about it?

- Who is involved? What is their background and are they newsworthy?

- Can you quote any statistics that confirm the case? For example, the latest national road traffic accident statistics would be useful to charities involved in road safety.

- Local links. Where are you based and what links do you have with the local community?

- What is the rest of your organization involved with? Previous successes? Current trends?

Ten final tips for copywriters

1. Work out what to say, then say it. The simplest route is usually the best.

2. Cut your first draft by half, then halve it again. Long copy sells, but not if it's too long for the space.

3. Think visual. Copy has to be seen before it gets read, and a picture can be worth a thousand words.

4. Make the style fit the subject. Make the style fit the medium. Make the style fit the audience.

5. The shorter the words, the clearer the message.

6. A relevant quote from a relevant source is worth more than all your deathless prose.

7. Think first, write later. Thinking as you write makes for long, muddled copy.

8. Get it right. You have to know the rules before you can break them creatively.

9. Read it again in the morning, preferably aloud. Confusion and double meanings will creep in.

10. Forget your Booker Prize hopes. Copywriting is a craft, not an art.

Useful reference works

Books

Every writer should have access, in book form, to:

- An up-to-date dictionary (do not rely on the spellcheck on your PC).

- A thesaurus. Your aim should be to wear it out within two years. The computer-based thesaurus that came with your PC does not contain enough words.

- Dictionaries of quotations (very useful for livening up text).

- A book on grammar and English usage. Other titles in this series are useful, and I would also recommend *Everyday Grammar* by John Seely (OUP, 2001).

- An encyclopedia or gazetteer (very useful for checking proper names).

- Literary companions (again, very useful for checking).

- A book of dates, anniversaries and names. Several exist, very useful for spotting anniversaries—can be an interesting way to start copy.

- An up-to-date copy of the *Writers' and Artists' Yearbook*, published annually by A. & C. Black.

- *Cassell's Directory of Publishing*, published annually.

Press guides

Willings Press Guide: volume i covers the UK, volume ii is international. Annual publication, available from: Media Information Ltd, Chess House, 34 Germain Street, Chesham, Bucks HP5 1SJ; telephone 0870 7360015. Website: willingspressguide.com

BRAD: monthly guide to advertising media, available from EMAP Business Communications Ltd, Bowling Green Lane, London EC1R ODA; telephone 020 7505 8458

The World of Learning: annual guide to all museums, galleries, libraries, archives, and colleges, worldwide coverage. Available from Europa Publications, 11 New Fetter Lane, London EC4P 4EL

Directories of Associations: UK and international, available from CBD Research Ltd, 15 Wickham Place, Beckenham, Kent BR3 5JS; telephone 020 8650 7745

Useful websites

The Writers' Site: contains both the Society of Authors and the Writers' Guild of Great Britain. www.writers.org.uk; www.writers.org.uk/society/; www.writers.org.uk/guild/

Permissions

Extracts on pp. 9 and 36 taken from Peter Hobday, *Managing the Message* (London House, 2000).
Press release on p. 43 with thanks to Stephanie Allen, and John Murray publishers.

Index